Smith College

THE CAMPUS GUIDE

Smith College

AN ARCHITECTURAL TOUR BY

Margaret Birney Vickery

PHOTOGRAPHS BY

Bilyana Dimitrova

WITH AN ESSAY BY

Nina Antonetti

FOREWORD BY

Carol T. Christ

Princeton Architectural Press

NEW YORK | 2007

Princeton Architectural Press
37 East Seventh Street
New York, New York 10003

For a free catalog of books, call 1.800.722.6657.
Visit our website at www.papress.com.

All photographs © Bilyana Dimitrova, unless
otherwise noted.

Image credits:
Smith College Archives: pages 1 bottom (photograph
by Knowlton Brothers), 2, 4, 6 (photograph by
James A. Langone), 10 (photograph by J. W.
Heffernan), 17 (F. L. Olmstead and Co.), 18 (John
Nolan), 22 (photograph by Eric Stahlberg), 94 and
124 (Fish/Parham)
Progressive Architecture: page 7
Bohlin Cywinski Jackson: page 11
Botanic Garden of Smith College: pages 15 (photo-
graph by Madelaine Zadik), 19 left, 19 right

(photograph by Jim Gipe), 21 left, 21 right (photo-
graph by Madelaine Zadik), 23 (photograph by
Madelaine Zadik), 24 (photograph by Philip
Channing), 25 (photograph by Sheri Lyn Peabody)
Margaret Birney Vickery: page 66 left

Series editor: Nancy Eklund Later
Series concept: Dennis Looney
Project editor and layout: Nicola Bednarek
Maps: Matt Knutzen

Special thanks to:
Nettie Aljian, Sara Bader, Dorothy Ball, Janet
Behning, Becca Casbon, Penny (Yuen Pik) Chu,
Russell Fernandez, Pete Fitzpatrick, Sara Hart, Jan
Haux, Clare Jacobson, John King, Mark Lamster,
Linda Lee, Katharine Myers, Lauren Nelson Packard,
Scott Tennent, Jennifer Thompson, Joseph Weston,
and Deb Wood of Princeton Architectural Press
                              —Kevin Lippert, publisher

Library of Congress Cataloging-in-Publication Data:
Vickery, Margaret Birney, 1963–
  Smith college : the campus guide : an architectural
tour / by Margaret Birney Vickery ; photographs by
Bilyana Dimitrova ; with an essay by Nina Antonetti ;
foreword by Carol T. Christ.
    p. cm.
  Includes bibliographical references and index.
  ISBN-13: 978-1-56898-591-6 (alk. paper)
  ISBN-10: 1-56898-591-6 (alk. paper)
  1. Smith College—Buildings. I. Title.
  LD7154.V53 2007
  378.744'23—dc22
                                              2006030351

This book is intended for visitors, alumnae/i, and students who wish to have an insider's look at the Smith College campus, from Peabody & Stearns's College Hall of 1876, to Skidmore, Owings & Merrill's 1957 Cutter and Ziskind Houses, to Weiss/Manfredi Architects' Campus Center of 2003.

The guide opens with an introduction that discusses major architectural trends on campus in a historical context. The introduction is followed by an essay that analyzes the rich landscape architecture of the Smith campus, which has been a defining feature of its character throughout the college's history. The architectural tour consists of five walks covering sixty-seven buildings. Each building is illustrated and discussed within its architectural and social context and tied to the evolution of the college. A three-dimensional map identifies the buildings on the walk.

Visitors are welcome to tour the Smith campus:

Please call (413) 584-2700 or visit www.smith.edu for more information.

Acknowledgments

I would like to thank President Carol T. Christ for her generous support of this project. Nanci Young, the college archivist, whose knowledge of Smith College is limitless, has been an invaluable resource. Cheryl Obremski at the Physical Plant has been wonderfully helpful, providing plans and information about recent renovations. I thank Laurie Fenlason, executive director of public affairs, for her insightful comments on the text. Nina Antonetti has been helpful through it all. Thanks also to Helen Searing, professor emerita of art, for her informative emails, and William Brandt, director of campus operations and facilities, for his help with the new engineering and science building. Nancy Eklund Later and Nicola Bednarek have been patient and understanding editors. Peter, Oliver, Pixie, and Arthur Vickery have been wonderful and supportive. Many thanks to Emily Louko, without whom this project would not have happened.

Margaret Birney Vickery

I would like to thank members of the landscape studies steering committee, as well as Madelaine Zadik and David Osepowicz, for their help with the essay on the Smith campus landscape.

Nina Antonetti

Back of President's House

Smith College's founders had a weighty sense not only that they were creating a new college but that they were choosing a place for it. Northampton, with its assets of civic life, commerce, and natural beauty, was ultimately deemed "the best place." President Seelye spoke of the mountains whose summits define the campus's southwesterly vista as pedagogical partners in the new enterprise, "unsalaried professors, whose lessons richly supplement the poverty of our human teaching."

A sense of place defines who we are, and rarely more evocatively than in our college years. When we are living away from home for the first time, the choices we make, the intellectual passions we discover, and the friendships we form have a defining authority and resonance. Smith alumnae feel a powerful attachment to their campus. When connecting with one another, they speak first of their ties to place. "What house did you live in?" invariably precedes any question about graduation year or academic major. The landscape, the prospects, resonate as well; decades later, alumnae vividly recall a favorite route to class or the beauty of Paradise Pond.

While early women's colleges were envisioned as seminaries on a hill, Smith arose out of a different impulse: not to set women apart from the world but to anchor them in its rhythms and engagements. Students lived in family-style cottages that the college purchased from local citizens. They studied in Northampton's public library and worshiped in its churches. Today, the college literally opens its doors to the town, with atriums in the Brown Fine Arts Center and the Campus Center drawing visitors from Elm Street into the heart of the campus. The Grécourt Gates, visible from Main Street, are not barriers but beacons, symbols of Smith in the world.

No single style or aesthetic dominates Smith's architecture; its houses and halls are united in their diversity and eclecticism, animated by a commitment to design that is right for its time and resilient to the test of time. The campus's compact footprint—125 contiguous acres—affords the visitor an experience of a remarkable variety of architectural traditions on even the shortest walk. Many prospective students recount a powerful moment of encounter with the campus that sealed their desire to matriculate at Smith.

Whether looking out a window at the president's house or walking past Neilson Library, I am always conscious of others who have stood here before me or walked these same paths, gazing toward these same mountains, over many of the same rooflines, in the same seasonal light. Across the span of history, through innovation and preservation, expansion and consolidation, what defines Smith as a community is an intensely and gratefully shared sense of place.

Carol T. Christ
President, Smith College

TOP: *Paradise Pond*
BOTTOM: *View of Smith College campus, 1883*

Introduction

Smith College sits on the brow of a hill overlooking the city of Northampton to the east and the Holyoke Range to the south and west. The historic district of Elm Street, lined with historical homes, cuts through the northeastern side of campus. Surrounded by natural and architectural beauty, Smith College blends graciously with its surroundings. Tall, sheltering trees shade the paths that meander past Smith's Victorian residences and modern buildings, and the botanic gardens or Paradise Pond offer places for repose. Smith's first president, L. Clark Seelye (1875–1910), wanted an arboretum within the college, in order for students to learn from their surroundings. As the college has grown, not only does the wide assortment of plantings provide lessons in botany, but a study of its buildings offers a comprehensive course on American architecture from the eighteenth century to the present.

Smith's Victorian Beginnings

> I would have the education suited to the mental and physical wants of women. It is not my design to render my sex any the less feminine, but to develop as fully as may be the powers of womanhood, and furnish women with the means of usefulness, happiness, and honor, now withheld from them.[1]
>
> —Sophia Smith

Sophia Smith's aspirations for her college were fully realized in the last quarter of the nineteenth century. But the decision to found a women's college was not easy for her. By all accounts Smith was a shy and retiring woman. Unmarried, she lived with her sister and brother in Hatfield, Massachusetts, inheriting her brother Austin's fortune when he died in 1861. Unsure what to do with the results of her brother's frugality and sound investing, she consulted Hatfield's new young pastor, the Rev. John M. Greene, who suggested she found an academy in Hatfield, give money to Amherst College (he was a graduate), or endow Mount Holyoke Seminary, which his wife Louisa Dickinson Greene had attended. Instead Smith, who was hard of hearing, decided to found a school for the deaf and mute. But, in 1868, John Clark established the Clark School for the Deaf in Northampton, and Smith had to think again about what her legacy would be. There is some dispute as to who first suggested the higher education of women as a charitable cause. In his journal entries from the time, Greene recounted counseling Smith to think of women, proposing an alternative to the seminary model.

Whether it was entirely Greene's urgings, her own sympathies, or a combination of the two, by 1870 Smith had rewritten her will with instructions

Sophia Smith

to found a college for women in Northampton. Supportive of her plan and its Northampton location was George W. Hubbard, a close advisor to Smith who had drafted her will and went on to become one of the first trustees of the college. After Smith's death in 1870, Greene, together with other trustees named in the will, including William S. Tyler, professor of classics at Amherst, and Julius Seelye, also a professor at Amherst who later became Amherst's president in 1876, began to organize and structure this new venture in women's education. The college officially opened in 1875 with L. Clark Seelye as president and fourteen young women as its first students.

From the very beginning, Smith College offered an education to women that was equal to that for men, honoring and recognizing women's equal intellectual abilities. In this way it differed from its other early sisters, such as Vassar and Wellesley, which accommodated women not prepared for the full college course. Smith also broke with the architectural precedent set at Mount Holyoke, Vassar, and Wellesley. In these schools women lived, ate, and studied under one great roof. In contrast, both Seelye and Greene favored small dwellings, which would "be conducted as far as possible like well-ordered private homes" and would be sited around a central academic building.[2] Noted historian Helen Horowitz writes of the prevalent fears in the nineteenth century of women isolated from society. It was thought that they became too involved in intense friendships with one another, which were considered unhealthy for society as a whole.[3] Such fears, together with warnings from physicians about the dangers to women's health from overworking their brains, meant that the cottage system, with its domestic structure, could best promise to "preserve, develop and perfect womanly characteristics."[4]

The first buildings erected on campus reflect Smith's, Seelye's, and Greene's ambitions for their institution. The public spaces of College, Pierce, and Lilly halls are testaments to the academic ambitions of the founders. As a first student residence Dewey House was bought in 1871. Between 1876 and 1879 the firm of Peabody & Stearns was hired to build three new residences as well as College and Pierce halls. While this Boston firm designed many public buildings, they are perhaps best known for their domestic work, especially in the popular shingle style, epitomized in the house they built on Elm Street for the Clark family (which we know today as Clark Hall). Yet their residences at Smith are not typical of their domestic work, but show the influence of Alfred Waterhouse, in whose office Robert Peabody had studied in England. Waterhouse served for thirty years as the architect for Girton College, Cambridge, the first purpose-built college for women in England, which Seelye singled out in his *Early History* as a model for Smith. The founder of Girton, Emily Davies, shared Sophia Smith's belief that the curriculum in a women's college should mirror that of men's colleges. And she and Waterhouse also relied on the domestic example for their early buildings, in order to counter the same fears about women and education that Seelye faced in America.

The architectural connection between Girton's Old Hall and Smith's Hatfield or Hubbard houses is clearly evident. All three employ red brick with stone dressing, steep gables, and cheerful dormer windows. Patterned brickwork adds details in the gables. While the overall effect is quite similar to Girton, welcoming entrance porches and shutters around the windows on Hatfield, Hubbard, and Washburn are characteristic of American architecture.

The work of Smith's second architect, William Brockelsby, also relies on British architectural examples such as the Queen Anne and the Old English styles employed in Tyler and Albright houses. The Queen Anne style was very popular in English women's colleges, especially Newnham, which, like Girton, is affiliated with Cambridge University. Indeed, the architect of Newnham, Basil Champneys, asserted that the Queen Anne was what he called a "Domestic Collegiate" style, just right for women's colleges.[5] The cottage system at Smith proved very popular and influenced building at Mount Holyoke, Wellesley, and Bryn Mawr in the late nineteenth and early twentieth centuries.

In 1892, seventeen years after it opened, the college hired landscape architect Frederick Law Olmsted to lay out the campus. Olmsted created a parklike setting with winding paths connecting houses to each other and a series of irregularly shaped lawns surrounded by copses of trees leading down to College Lane. The results of his plan that we still see today are the paths that snake through the campus, connecting residences and academic buildings. By avoiding formal axes and rigid geometry Olmsted intended the college to grow like a pastoral village. Over a century later, the Smith campus still has an idyllic feel with its lush lawns, gracious trees, and spectacular views of Paradise Pond, the Mill River, and the hills beyond. While large building projects have helped Smith maintain its outstanding academic reputation, the preservation of the small-scale house system fostered a warm, welcoming atmosphere that is classic to Smith.

By the early twentieth century new academic buildings were being erected to meet the needs of the college. Enrollment had steadily increased and by 1910 numbered almost two thousand. The new projects continued to be built in the red brick of the early buildings, but a classical vocabulary was now introduced. The neo-classicism of the early twentieth century was popular on college campuses because of its associations with early American architecture as seen at Harvard and in the work of Charles Bulfinch. The additional benefit of this style was that it was considerably less expensive to build than the more ornate gothic. The classical vocabulary was first evident in Seelye Hall (1899) with its symmetrical layout, columns, and pilasters. But its active and energetic surface of contrasting stone and brick is still somewhat Victorian in feel. More true to classical roots are John M. Greene Hall (1910) and the Neilson Library (1909). While these are visually very different, they are both formal, symmetrical buildings that rely on classical motifs for their details. In 1914 President Marion L. Burton (1910–17) hired John Nolan, a landscape architect from Cambridge, Massachusetts, to draw up plans for the college. Burton had visions of enlarging Smith from a college to a university, and the plans Nolan presented reflected this goal. By razing some buildings and adding to others, he sought to bring what he called "order" to the campus.[6] His plans involved strong axial vistas and distinct symmetrical lawns surrounded by new and old buildings. Fences were to surround the campus, clearly defining its boundaries. While these ideas are characteristic of many campus plans, they would have dramatically altered the intimate scale of Smith as we know it. In its early years Smith's growth was organic, which was complemented by Olmsted's landscape plan. To assert such rigid confines on the campus would have felt artificial and detracted from the way Smith's growth harmonized with the natural beauty surrounding it.

Nolan's plan called for an official entrance to the college. While this was never implemented, the college did erect the Grécourt Gates in 1924. These cast-iron gates framed by red brick and stone walls serve as the symbolic

Grécourt Gates

entrance to the college. Originally on Elm Street, across from Northrop and Gillett houses, they were moved just below College Hall in 1953. The gates were built by the trustees to honor the work of a small band of Smith alumnae who worked in the village of Grécourt, France during World War I. At the urgings of Harriet Boyd, class of 1892, the alumnae raised $30,000 to send the Smith College Relief Unit abroad with supplies, where the women helped the villagers find food, water, clothing, and shelter between 1917 and 1920. As Dean Ada Comstock (1912–23) so eloquently stated:

> These gates, . . . which commemorated this service must never be regarded as gates of seclusion, of segregation, of protection. They form a wide gateway through which the graduates of this College will go out year by year as ready as the members of the Unit to dedicate all that they have to the common lot.[7]

The Grécourt Gates continue to represent a symbolic link between the college and the world beyond.

The only aspect of Nolan's ideas that was implemented was the large dormitory complex that he planned on Allen Field, across Paradise Road, today known as the Quadrangle. Both President Neilson (1917–39) and Dean Comstock were concerned about the housing situation for students, which they considered unfair and undemocratic. When Neilson took over in 1917, only 870 students lived in campus housing, 39 lived at home, and 1,084 were accommodated in surrounding boarding houses. In the November 1919 issue of the *Smith Alumnae Quarterly*, Comstock presented what she saw as the most urgent need of the college: equal housing for all its students. At the time there was great disparity in the system of boarding houses. Some were invitation-only houses, costing up to $650 per year and providing luxurious accommodations. Other houses were much more sparse and cost only $275 per year. Not only was cost an issue, but students lived with others of like financial means and often never met other students from different houses, different years, or different social strata. Comstock reasoned that only if the college took over the responsibility of housing all its students could a more equitable and socially beneficial system prevail.

The dean's plans for better housing included not just a room, or half a room per student, but also kitchenettes so students could offer hospitality to their friends as well as reception rooms, in which women could entertain visitors. She stressed that such requirement were not luxuries but

> instruments in education in the art of living. They should be provided for all students, not a fraction, and they should be provided at the lowest possible rate. We need direct supervision of the living arrangements of all our students so that we may offer equal opportunities to all; and this equality of

Postcard with aerial view of the campus, ca. 1910

opportunity is important not merely for the sake of the material benefits thereby conferred upon each student. It is highly important just as a matter of uniformity—of democracy.[8]

As the Quadrangle grew, it provided an axial order and formality that was new to the campus. It is a beautiful, unified group of buildings, which are tied to other buildings at Smith such as Northrop and Gillett houses through the use of red brick and white trim and various classical details. Their style is often referred to as neo-Georgian, a revival of a classical style of architecture popular in England in the seventeenth and eighteenth centuries, which is characterized by the use of red brick, with classical details such as columns, pilasters, and pediments of white stone or wood adding contrast. It relies on symmetry and a classical vocabulary for its elegance and modest grandeur.

By 1936, when King and Scales houses were opened and the Quad was completed, the campus had grown considerably. The smaller scale of the original buildings, with their steep gables and quaint dormers, had been replaced by a formal architectural vocabulary that was more collegiate than domestic—appropriate for what was then, and remains today, the largest college for women in the country.

The Arrival of the Modern Movement on Campus

The transition from a traditional style of architecture on campus as seen in the neo-Georgian Quadrangle or Sage Hall to the modern movement was not an easy one for Smith in the 1940s and 1950s. As early as 1939 historical details were omitted in the addition to the library and simple sandstone cladding replaced more traditional ornament. But the world was abuzz with the new International Style, which celebrated the barest bones of a building and the simple honesty of the modern materials of steel, glass, and concrete.

Winning design of dormitory competition by Norman C. Fletcher, Jean Bodman Fletcher, and Benjamin Thompson, 1946

Modern architects saw historicism as out of place in the twentieth century, and by the end of World War II, the college had caught on to this trend and decided to try something altogether new architecturally.

In 1946 the college teamed up with the magazine *Pencil Points* and the Museum of Modern Art to offer a competition for new dormitories. It was hoped that young architects, early in their careers, would enter. The jury—including William Allen Neilson, president emeritus; Kenneth Reid, editor of *Pencil Points*; trustee Lucia Valentine (née Norton, class of 1923); the architects Philip Goodwin and Morris Ketchum; and Elizabeth Mock, curator of architecture at the Museum of Modern Art—looked for designs that best fit the college's parklike setting, that would provide ample sunlight in students' rooms, that would harmonize with existing buildings on campus and Elm Street, and that would not seem institutional.[9]

The winning designs by Norman C. Fletcher, Jean Bodman Fletcher, and Benjamin Thompson clearly illustrate the influence of Walter Gropius, one of the fathers of the modern movement, and the Bauhaus. The drawings show a series of flat-roofed, rectangular blocks, clad in brick (not the red brick of the campus), with large banks of glass windows set within the structural supports. The main building, in the winning view, rests on slender columns with space for bike storage on the ground floor and living spaces beginning on the second floor, giving the effect of a building floating above the ground. Glazed connectors link nearby units with each other. The buildings, sleek and ideologically pure, are thoroughly modern, with no references to traditional architecture.

The outcry from the alumnae was voluble and immediate. By May 1946, a month after the designs were published, President Herbert John Davis (1940–49) and trustee Lucia Valentine were corresponding with and visiting the architects, who by this time were working together in Gropius's office in

Cambridge, to find a compromise that would console the alumnae. The letters from Valentine to Davis recounting these meetings give a marvelous view into the architectural world of the 1940s. Because of their committed ideology to the new style of architecture, which for them symbolized a new world, the architects rejected suggestions from Davis and Valentine such as brick cladding that sympathized with other brick buildings nearby. For example, "A pitched roof over the living room-dining room unit filled them with repulsion," Valentine wrote.[10] Gropius would brook no compromise. The architects, according to Valentine, could not understand the pressure Smith was under to introduce "acceptable modern architecture" while appeasing the influential alumnae at the same time.[11] She finished her letter:

> I will confess that I am sick at heart about the whole affair and wish we were well out of it, not because of the protests against modern architecture but because I sincerely wonder whether this firm is capable of escaping modern clichés and Bauhaus mannerisms and developing a beautiful, friendly building.[12]

These difficulties persisted, and in 1949, when Davis left the college there was still no resolution to the dormitory problem.

In 1955 Lamont House was built to relieve some of the overcrowding. The traditional, neo-Georgian style in which it was clad ruffled few feathers but disappointed those who wished to see some truly contemporary modern architecture on campus. Two years later, Cutter and Ziskind houses were opened and marked a turning point in Smith's architecture. Designed by Skidmore, Owings & Merrill (SOM), they epitomize the International Style so popular at the time and introduced the college to the modern movement. This time the trustees and president Wright remained committed to SOM's modern designs and fended off alumnae criticism, arguing that Smith had always built in the style of the day and should continue to do so. Contemporary styles of architecture became the norm in the buildings that followed, from the Clark Science Center (1966) to the Friedman Complex (1978) and the Ainsworth Gymnasium (1977).

Historic Preservation and Postmodernism

As new buildings arrived on campus in the late 1960s and early 1970s several old structures were sacrificed. In the course of constructing the new art building by John Andrews (1972), which many may remember for its Brutalist style of architecture, the old president's house, Gateway, was razed, as were Hillyer Hall, Graham Hall, and the Tryon Art Gallery. The loss of these buildings raised a modest outcry from faculty who believed that Gateway in particular should be saved. But when the Alumnae Gymnasium (1891) was threatened to make way for a large new wing of the library, the calls to preserve this architectural gem were organized and persistent. In the early 1970s the practice of historic preservation was just emerging. Several Smith alumnae were pioneers in the field and in 1975, together with other alumnae and faculty, they mounted a huge campaign to save Alumnae Gym. Moves were made to register the building with the National Register of Historic Places, citing both its architectural beauty as well as its historic importance as the site of the first women's basketball game as reasons for its place on the register. A grant from the National Trust for Historic Preservation was received to help fund a feasibility study to look into ways to save and reuse the building. The commitment of those alumnae dedicated to saving Alumnae Gym has become embedded in the collective psyche of the campus. The architectural past of the nineteenth and early twentieth centuries is now recognized as an integral part of Smith and with that recognition has come a commitment to preserve.

Complementary to the goals of historic preservation was the postmodern movement in architecture. In October 1985 the architectural firm of Shepley, Bulfinch, Richardson and Abbott, who had previously built the McConnell and Sabin-Reed halls in the 1960s, were hired to renovate the existing science buildings and design a new one. Yvonne Freccero, director of planning and research, stressed that this addition not only function well as a science building but that it should be "an attractive addition to the whole campus. . . . It must be seen as a connection not a barrier."[13] Plans proceeded, and by 1991 the new Bass Hall and Young Science Library were opened. These buildings were the first in almost forty years to deliberately borrow architectural features from the past. Here, a traditional architectural vocabulary including stringcourses, columns, pitched roofs, and gables are used in sometimes quirky or whimsical ways but echoing motifs found on older buildings. The use of warm red brick ties the new science center to its predecessors from the 1960s.

Recent Buildings and Smith's Future

In recent years several exciting new buildings have opened at Smith College, including the Olin Fitness Center, the Brown Fine Arts Center, and the Campus Center. All three graciously nod to their older architectural neighbors without borrowing from them. As postmodernism has waned in popularity, architects are acknowledging precedents while remaining thoroughly contemporary. For example, the Campus Center (2003) snakes through a narrow site, like the meandering path it was built over, and uses board-and-batten siding. Both elements tie it to the past in abstract ways. In the Brown Fine Arts Center, the tradition of red brick is continued, and the areas of patterned brickwork are reminiscent of buildings such as College and Pierce halls. In all cases the architects sought to complement Smith's historical setting while saying something new.

As these building campaigns have been going on across campus, the college has continued its commitment to preservation, renovating and upgrading dozens of older buildings around campus. With new energy-efficient windows and subtle additions, which make them accessible to all, they refresh Smith's historic past. President Carol T. Christ (2002–present) is a committed custodian of this rich heritage and plans for Smith's future with care and deliberation. Within this process, the new engineering and science building figures largely. As Smith takes the lead in engineering at women's colleges, the program will be housed in a spectacular and progressive building designed by the architectural firm of Bohlin Cywinski Jackson.

Two highly significant features stand out in the plans for this new building. The first is its location across Green Street on the corner of Belmont Avenue. This site has been controversial because it will greatly change the face of Green Street and displace tenants in three Smith-owned apartment houses. Over the past few years, Smith has been providing replacement housing in downtown Northampton for those residents who have to move. It should also be remembered that Green Street has changed radically over the last one hundred years, from a leafy residential street to a blend of residential, commercial, and academic buildings, culminating in the Mendenhall Center for the Performing Arts (1968) and Sage Hall (1924).

The new Engineering and Science Building is also to be a tangible expression of the college's commitment to a sustainable future at Smith. The building will feature sophisticated methods of charting and controlling energy use, new technologies for power conversion, and will be an important

Green Street, n.d.

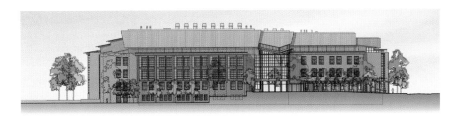

Engineering and Science Building, east elevation

educational and research tool for students, faculty, and the wider community. With enthusiastic support from one of its major donors, the Ford Motor Company, it will sport a green roof, which will help control run-off, cool the building in the summer, and insulate it in the colder months. The new building will be designed, constructed, and will function with the environment in mind and is expected to be certified at the silver or gold level by Leadership in Energy and Environmental Design (LEED). Early sketches show it clad in red brick to tie it to its neighbors, with plenty of glass to provide natural lighting.

The elements of sustainable design integral to this building are also integral to Smith's vision of the future. President Christ has organized a Committee on Sustainability with the aim of developing a plan for sustainability on campus. As this evolves, the college is soon to open a co-generation plant that will produce steam for both heating and electricity, saving the college some $650,000 per year and cutting greenhouse gases by almost half. This project, together with greater efforts at conservation, will both save the college money and help to conserve our natural resources.

President Christ emphasized the importance of these programs in an article in 2005:

> We believe strongly in developing the campus in ways that assure long-term sustainability in our use of resources.... There's an obvious and increasing need in today's world for institutions, as well as individuals, to become aware of our impact on the earth and its resources and to make every effort to behave with responsibility toward the environment.[14]

The new engineering and science building will be not just an architectural statement about Smith's concern for our environmental future. It will serve as an important and vital tool in educating students in the environmental sciences and sustainable design.

With the burgeoning engineering program and construction of its new home, Smith is once again leading the way in women's education. While the campus has changed drastically from 1875 with its three buildings placed in front of cow pastures, its commitment to women's higher education has been unfaltering. An architectural tour of Smith begins with an academic building surrounded by small houses and ends with a look at the needs of the global community.

The landscape of Smith College represents the visions of the college founders, the designs of notable architects and landscape architects, the desires of the community, the pedagogical needs of the curriculum, and the memories of alumnae. Its conception signaled a pivotal moment in women's history, as few places before had been so purposefully designed to benefit women. Sophia Smith, the benefactress; L. Clark Seelye, the inaugural president; and Peabody & Stearns, the initial architects; among others, sought to create a campus appropriate for Victorian women undertaking a college education. Whereas their mission to educate women—to offer a liberal arts curriculum comparable to nearby Amherst College—was progressive, never-theless their resolution to house women with local families rather than board them in large dormitories adhered to traditional notions of women in society. Even when the house system moved onto campus in cottages purchased or built for that purpose, the administration was relegating students to the home. Today the nurturing effects of a domestic environment have proven to benefit rather than belie the rigors of the academic mission, and conse-quently, the house system has been called the heart of Smith College.

The campus then is its lungs. This landscape is charged with duality: the pastoral aesthetic represents privilege and yet the student body is one of the most economically and racially diverse among its peer institutions; the

Camperdown elm in winter, Ulmus glabra

scientific significance of this arboretum-campus educates women in the art of design; the eclecticism of architectural styles consistently follows the trajectory of changing tastes in high art; the grounds are nestled within the Pioneer Valley but situated on a brow overlooking Northampton; the landscape frames views and vistas in nearly every direction, and yet is subordinated to the placement of its buildings. Landscape architects Mark Francis and Randy Hester would remind us that "In [a] garden these apparent irreconcilables are clarified and mediated because the garden accepts paradox."[1] The complexity of the landscape at Smith hosts a variety of experiences, mirroring the scope and breadth of perspectives offered by this distinguished community and its curriculum.

Even before the Olmsted Plan of 1893, the site had good bones, enhanced by several of New England's wonders, most notably the Holyoke Range, Mount Tom, and the Connecticut River and its rich floodplains. For Smith, the real estate adage is true: "location, location, location." The campus is naturally terraced, stepping down 120 feet from the eastern side of Elm Street to the banks of Paradise Pond and the Mill River. These delineations within the natural landscape have influenced the overall design of the campus, defining space and dramatizing views. As a constructed landscape, the campus recapitulates the triumphs and tribulations fundamental to landscape history in this country as values changed, styles evolved, botany advanced, and intellectual debates endured. Its physical identity is born from the concept of the house system rather than an overriding architectural style or building material, providing an alternative to the collegiate cohesion found at nearby Mount Holyoke College or Yale. The kaleidoscopic effect provides insight into the history and evolution of the site—the remnants of the local silk mill industry are still visible in the rerouting of waterways and train tracks around the periphery of the campus; the shadows of nineteenth-century social reform can be detected in the ruins of the state hospital hovering behind the athletic fields; the trends in architectural styles, from the English-inspired Queen Anne revival to the minimalism of the post-war era International Style to recent examples of contemporary design, are scattered throughout the campus; and, perhaps most poignantly, the evolution of women's education can be discerned in the housing patterns and shifting academic emphasis.

In the beginning, the campus was a means by which to control, protect, nurture, and instruct women as they embarked on higher education.[2] The decision to house students with families in town and then in houses on campus enabled the administration and staff to keep a watchful eye on them and provide a domestic environment in which to temper the independence that might otherwise have come with educational opportunity. College officials believed that smaller buildings and the pastoral aesthetic would provide appropriate settings for the cultivation of womanhood:

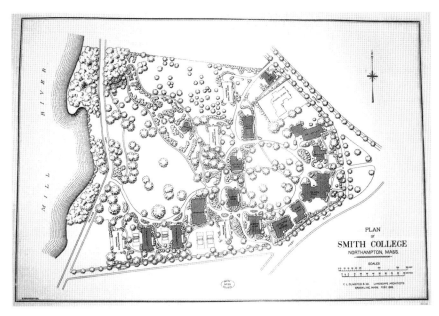

Landscape master plan by Law Olmsted, 1893

> Our two thousand girls should live, so far as we can determine it, in the most advantageous atmosphere for their intellectual and spiritual and physical development. We want not to accustom them to luxury but to accustom them to beautiful surroundings. We have…a great gift of nature in our landscape. We have done a great deal toward making that landscape visible from as many points of view on the campus as possible, so that the natural beauty will be brought to bear on the girl day by day. We have, in making over old houses and in the planning of new houses, tried to let the student see that you can live indoors in surroundings that will constantly give impressions, if not of positive beauty, at least of the absence of ugliness, so that you do not have the shock of coming from the hills around here into things of the kind that distress any soul sensitive to beauty.[3]

The success of the Olmsted Plan of 1893 relies not only on the beauty but also the intellectual opportunities it affords students. President Seelye recognized the importance of the landscape as a teaching tool and campaigned for an arboretum, whose splendor has brought great distinction to Smith.

Frederick Law Olmsted is central to the history of the Smith College campus, which was founded one generation after Olmsted and Calvert Vaux launched the landscape architecture profession with their winning entry for Central Park. Smith's original master plan was created by Olmsted's firm the same year as another of its famous designs, the World's Columbian Exposition in Chicago. The concept for Olmsted's plan of 1893—featuring winding paths, framed views, expansive vistas, set within

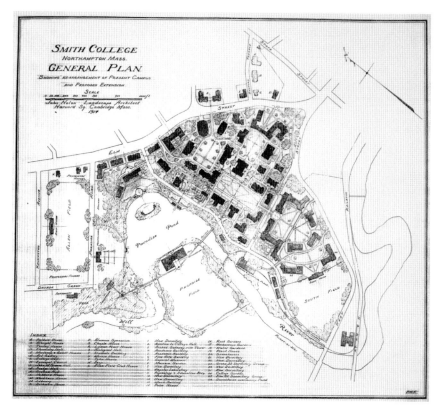

Landscape master plan by John Nolan, 1914

a residential scale—remains visible in many aspects of the campus, despite significant alterations, expansions, and modernizations throughout the ages.

Merely two decades later, President Marion L. Burton hired John Nolan, a Cambridge-based landscape architect, whose formal approach challenged Olmsted's footprint. In his 1914 plan, Nolan proposed tying disparate sections of the campus together into a neatly fenced and axially aligned package, marking an important juncture in the field of landscape architecture when the formality of early modernists was supplanting the informality of Olmsted's pastoral aesthetic. The resulting Quadrangle is an example of Nolan's approach: the collegiate architecture, archway, courtyards, and monumental scale provide a striking contrast to and are kept at arm's length from the rest of the campus.

This tension between formal and informal culminated in the mid-twentieth-century arrival of the International Style with the Cutter-Ziskind dormitories, which brought both modernism as a style and modern modes of living to Smith, notably on the other side of Elm Street. Although viewed by many as a departure from the otherwise New England character of Smith, this architectural complex dramatically expanded the architectural

LEFT: *Student on swing hanging in a sugar maple,* Acer saccharum, *overlooking Paradise Pond*
RIGHT: *Ruth Brown Richardson Memorial Garden with Lyman Conservatory in the background*

and landscape vocabulary of the campus and offers ongoing debates about tradition vs. innovation, old vs. new, domestic vs. foreign—topics otherwise relegated to the classroom and studio. Yet the style was very appropriate to the day and thereby reminiscent of Sophia Smith's request that all buildings be contemporary to their times. Although in this case, the architecture dominates the landscape, the International Style does indeed have great relevance in Massachusetts by way of Walter Gropius. After serving as the director of the Bauhaus in Germany, Gropius became dean of Harvard's Graduate School of Design in the 1930s and taught three particular students who rose through the ranks to become the reigning trio of modern landscape architects: Garrett Eckbo, Dan Kiley, and James Rose. They, along with Gropius, mentored the first generation of women to study at Harvard, many of whom were Smith graduates.

Since the Cutter-Ziskind era, developments on campus have continued to parallel professional debates within architecture and landscape architecture. The demolition of Hillyer and Tryon, which formed the original art complex, the threatened demise of Alumnae Gymnasium, and the new construction of the Campus Center have educated the community in prevailing theories regarding preservation, conservation, and style.[4] In their recent transformation of the Brown Fine Arts Center, Polshek and Rodriguez, of Polshek Partnership Architects, asserted:

Buildings, like humans, get old. Their systems break down, and their envelopes decay. They no longer fulfill dreams, respond to users' needs or express dominant ideas of their times....For the architect of a transformational project, the opportunity to create a new life out of an old one is like discovering an architectural fountain of youth. There is a kind of reassurance in utilizing the past to create a future, particularly when it is appropriate to substitute new imagery for old.[5]

Conversations, or even arguments, about the resulting landscape often seem richer than the events or buildings themselves, providing opportunities for students, faculty, administrators, and alumnae to advocate for the best interests of the campus as we attempt to preserve the past while moving forward. Although architecture has often dominated these discussions, the buildings, it must be remembered, are elements within a greater context, an academic landscape. Any changes to the former impact the latter.

In the 1990s, that recognition brought a concerted effort to readdress the transience of the campus in the face of large architectural projects and continued maintenance issues. John Burk, Gates Professor of Biological Sciences, on the centennial of the botanic garden, proposed:

The future raises new demands, requiring activities largely unforeseen a hundred years ago. The first of these involves conservation, focused research and public education devoted to maintaining healthy populations of plant species in their native habitats, an essential task if the garden is not to become a museum of living artifacts, extinct in the natural world. The second is a very different form of stewardship, the careful preservation, within each garden, of the remnants of its history, its connections with its past. At Smith College, the Botanic Garden is fortunate in still possessing landscapes with plantings that reflect the vision and intentions of the garden's founders a century ago. A critical part of the garden's mission in the future must be to keep these dreams intact.[6]

The gardens, much like the buildings, are elements of a whole, and to safeguard the collection is to preserve the sanctity of the entire campus.

To that end, Burk chaired the Landscape Master Plan Committee responsible for the landscape master plan of 1995, coauthored by Shavaun Towers (class of 1971) and Cornelia Hahn Oberlander (class of 1944). Towers and Oberlander penned a tripartite document to preserve and prepare the campus for the twenty-first century, including program and analysis, plan development, and a design manual. Their objective was rigorous:

Planning should be as much a creative exercise in preservation and enhancement as it is an exploration of development opportunities. A regard for the

LEFT: *Japanese Garden for Reflection and Contemplation*
RIGHT: *Ruth Brown Richardson Memorial Perennial Garden with Flanders poppies,* Papaver rhoeas, *in bloom*

past, the history and traditions of the institution, will inform the assessment of its future needs. An understanding of current problems and a recognition of potential assets will provide a sound basis for decisions regarding the allocation of resources to most efficiently create and maintain a physical environment which encourages and reflects the quality of the academic life of the College. The findings of this study should also foster the creation of a social environment of interaction and engagement.[7]

Towers and Oberlander reconsidered Olmsted's original 27 acres within the 125 acre-campus; reintroduced aspects of John Nolan's rejected plan, which now offered fresh insights and opportunities; and reconceived the role of the landscape in the aesthetic, scientific, and cultural life of the college. This met, if not surpassed, the charge of then president Mary Maples Dunn: "[The master plan] will bring to the campus spatial and visual harmony, informed by the intellectual and political energy of women entering the twenty-first century."[8]

Meanwhile, Susan Komroff (class of 1962), Paula Deitz (class of 1959), and Ann Leone (class of 1971) were busily pioneering the landscape studies program, whose steering committee John Burk joined. Together they launched what is considered to be the first program of its kind at an undergraduate liberal arts college in the States.[9]

Home Gardening class preparing beds near Capen House Gardens, 1924

Smith has a rich legacy in educating women in studies of the built environment. Plant courses have been offered since the founding of the college and the architecture studios have just celebrated their centennial. From the early days, when Smith was closely affiliated with the Cambridge School, which educated women in design when Harvard would not, through recent times, when the college launched the first engineering program at a women's college as well as the landscape studies program, Smith's campus has been a living laboratory for courses across the curriculum, from botany to architectural history. The loyalty of the student body to their landscape is also cultivated by particular traditions, such as the ceremonies of incoming students receiving a piece of ivy and of graduating seniors planting ivy, as well as the much heralded Illumination Night, when the campus is festooned with colorful lanterns the evening before commencement. These course offerings, traditions, and events instill allegiance and inspire stewardship among the Smith community.

Students study diverse habitats (plant, animal, mineral, and cultural) throughout the campus, including the horticulture of the labeled species of the arboretum, the ecology of the conservatory pond and Paradise Pond, the hydrology of the Mill River, the history of styles from various nations and periods, and the psychology of public, private, and sacred spaces. Students will also be able to study issues of sustainability and conservation with the arrival of the first roof garden at Smith, which will adorn the new science and engineering building, at the corner of Green Street and Belmont

Rock Garden with Lyman Conservatory in the background

Avenue. The roof garden will further expand the broad range of garden typologies on campus.

Of the many enduring treasures that collectively define the campus, such as the arboretum, plant house, water features, and sculpture, perhaps the gardens are most revered.[10] They include the Systematics Garden (1894, redesigned 1980s), Rock Garden (1897), Japanese Garden for Reflection and Contemplation (1986), Ruth Brown Richardson Perennial Border (1984), Wildflower and Woodland Garden (mid-1980s), Fern Garden (1978), President's Residence Garden (1920), and Capen Garden (1921, recently redesigned by Nancy Watkins Denig (class of 1968). The latter is the most formal example on campus, adhering to an axis, boasting a splendid knot garden, and providing outdoor classroom space for horticulture classes. The indoor classroom and laboratory spaces are located in the recently renovated and expanded Lyman Plant House, which is open to the public and includes an audio walking tour.

What connects all these disparate spaces is the compelling collection of trees, all carefully labeled as exhibits within the arboretum. They are the most prominent legacy of a remarkable botanical garden staff, dating back to the first director, Professor William Ganong, who "was an innovative educator and influenced how botany was taught across the country, authoring botany texts and developing special equipment for the scientific study of plants."[11] Other noteworthy staff include the horticulturalist William I. P. Campbell, whose tenure spanned four decades and coincided with the

Lyman Conservatory at night

hurricane of 1938, which felled more than two hundred campus trees, and Albert F. Blakeslee, who was a pioneer of chromosomal studies.

The splendors of the campus are punctuated by water features, including the picturesque pond beside the conservatory, the aptly named Paradise Pond and island, the Mill River and waterfall, the Lanning Fountain, and the fountain at Capen Garden. Sculptures throughout the campus landscape span the spectrum from representative to kinetic, often showcasing the work of distinguished faculty, such as *Owl* by Leonard Baskin (poised in front of Wright Hall, see page 45), a lifelike heron on the conservatory pond by Elliott Offner, and a lifelike horse at the entrance to the stables, also by Offner. Temporary installations have brought acclaim to this collection, especially when at the turn of the twenty-first century Patrick Dougherty, a.k.a. "Twig-man,"[12] built *Paradise Gates* with locally found materials and using volunteers from an eager college community. This assemblage piece on Burton Lawn, now gone, has left a lasting impression, as many recall "the stick castle."

The Smith College campus wears its jewelry—whether buildings, trees, rocks, a tea hut, a waterfall, or sculpture—well. As the famed landscape chronicler and practitioner Humphry Repton judiciously observed in the 1790s:

> The perfection of landscape gardening depends on a concealment of those operations of *art* by which *nature* is embellished; but where buildings are introduced, *art* declares herself openly, and should, therefore, be very careful, lest she have cause to blush at her interference.[13]

Lanning Fountain, with Systematics Garden and Lyman Conservatory in background

Indeed, Smith's landscape understands its place: it displays Victorian ornamentation with vitality, modernist minimalism with stoicism, and contemporary flair with aplomb. It possesses the aesthetics of Olmsted, the formality of Nolan, and the consciousness of Towers and Oberlander, while also offering instruction in the collections, contemplation in the beauty, and recreation in the expansiveness. Most importantly, this landscape models the past and anticipates the future, indicating the many paths each of us may choose to follow.

Belmont Avenue

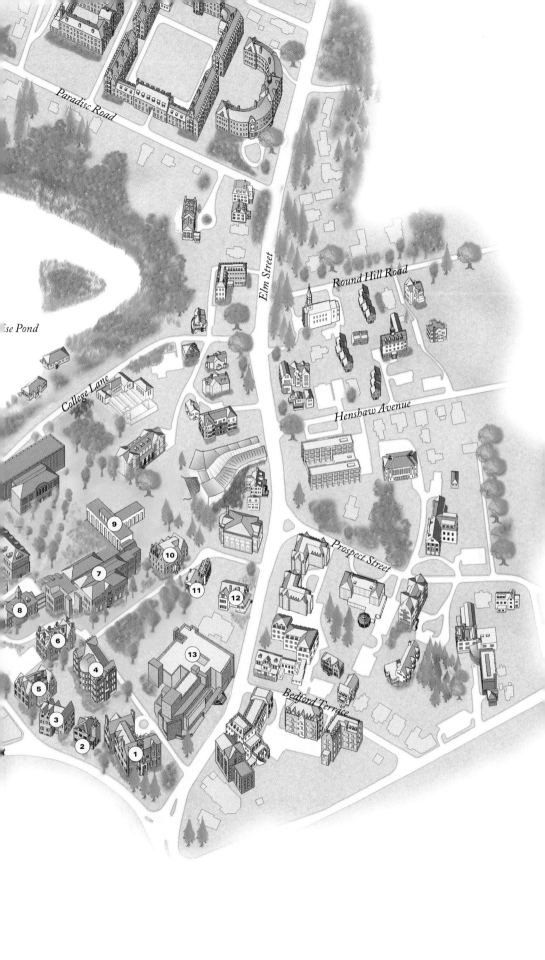

Paradise Road

ise Pond

Elm Street

Round Hill Road

College Lane

Henshaw Avenue

Prospect Street

Bedford Terrace

9

10

7

8

6

4

5

3

2

1

11

12

13

College Hall

1. College Hall   *Peabody & Stearns, 1875*

Addition   *1890*

College Hall, Smith's first building, was completed in 1875. It held the offices of the president and the college doctor as well as a large social hall, boudoir, and recitation rooms on the second floor, while on the first floor were lecture rooms, the treasurer's room, additional recitation rooms, as well as a "Ladies Reading and Dressing Room."[1] An art gallery was on the third floor. Early circulars stressed that the majority of rooms needed by the students on a regular basis were on the first floor and thus did not need to be accessed by stairs, which was considered a "safeguard" to women's health.[2] College Hall became the academic and social hub of the college, while the nearby cottages provided a domestic retreat for the students.

This purely academic building, erected in a place of prominence on a hill, mirrors what Seelye knew from Amherst and other men's colleges. The winning plans for the building (and for the president's house, Gateway, now demolished) were submitted by Peabody & Stearns from Boston. These were early commissions for Peabody & Stearns who went on to have a successful practice through the end of the century and into the early twentieth century. They built many great houses for the wealthy in the Berkshires and along the northern coast of Massachusetts, as well as commercial buildings from Boston to St. Louis. But in 1874, when they won the commission at Smith, they had only been in practice for a few years. One of their earliest works was Matthew's Hall (1871) at Harvard University, a large symmetrical dormitory of red brick with white stone dressing and Gothic details such as the entrance porches and the bay and oriel windows. While this work may have helped the architects to win the commission at Smith, equally influential may have been Robert Peabody's early training in 1869 in the office of Alfred Waterhouse, the architect of Girton, England's first women's college.

For College Hall, Peabody & Stearns designed a dramatic building of red brick. The facade is energized by arched and rectangular windows trimmed with white stone and divided by columns with foliated capitals. A great square clock tower, with a second-floor oriel window highlighting the president's suite within, lends the building an architectural drama that proclaims its importance to the college and town. College Hall illustrates the Victorians' love for an architecture of lively wall surfaces and bold silhouettes. While the eastern facade of College Hall overlooking Northampton has remained unchanged over the years, the western elevations have been altered, as have the interiors. An account by Ester Wyman, class of 1911, mentions a one-story wing off the rear of the building. This was the laboratory, built as only one story "so that if it blew up, damage to the rest of the building would be slight."[3] As the college grew rapidly, interior changes were made, especially to the Assembly Hall in order to accommodate more students for chapel and other events. In 1890 the laboratory wing was removed and a two-story transept addition with a three-arched entry porch was created. On the first floor a larger reading room resulted, while on the second floor the Assembly Hall could now accommodate nine hundred students. Smith College records do not cite the architect of this addition, but it is generally assumed to be by Peabody & Stearns.

By 1901 even more space was needed and the college removed the floor between the first and second floors, added galleries, and increased seating by about five hundred. Nine years later, when John M. Greene Hall was built, the floor was replaced and the hall was once again smaller and used for concerts and lectures. The space is now divided up into administrative offices.

Of the oak-paneled interiors much has changed. But the beautiful oak staircase remains, and the offices of the president and treasurer still give the visitor a glimpse of their nineteenth-century splendor. In 1949 a student criticized College Hall for lacking the "functionalism" so in vogue in the mid-twentieth century.[4] But in the early twenty-first century, the energetic facade with its warm red brick, asymmetrical massing, arched windows, and proud tower is considered an architectural treasure.

College Hall, Pierce Hall, and Lilly Hall

2. Pierce Hall   *Peabody & Stearns, 1882*

Addition and renovations   *Goody Clancy and Associates, 1995*

Pierce Hall, originally known as Music Hall, was built by Peabody & Stearns to house the Smith College School of Music. The building, devoted entirely to the study and practice of music, is situated just to the south of College Hall. Together with the Hillyer School of Art it was one of two new academic buildings opened in 1882, representing the college's wholehearted commitment to the disciplines of music and art.

While not as architecturally lively a building as College Hall, Music Hall continued the tradition of red brick, this time with red sandstone dressing around the windows, doorways, and in the details. The facade that looks inward toward the campus is particularly simple. At first glance the building appears to be a solid cube with a central entry marked by an arched doorway beneath a tall gable block. Most striking is the ocular window in the third-story gable. To the right of the central block is a shallow wing with decorative tile hanging and half-timbering in the third-story gable. These domestic details were borrowed from the Old English style and were preserved in the addition of 1995. In original photographs small, timbered dormer windows and vents soften and break up the otherwise expansive slate roof.

The facade facing West Street looks almost spartan on the first two floors, with windows that appear to be punched through the brick walls. But on the third floor a twin gable, now clad in clapboard but originally tile-hung, with a long bank of sash windows with half-timbering around them (now gone), suggests a certain domesticity. The entrance on the east side of the building is beneath a deep, sheltering porch, supported on stubby sandstone columns with foliated capitals and decorated by a timber screen.

The addition in 1995 of a staircase tower echoes the eastern tower on West Street. Here the architects, Goody Clancy and Associates, a Boston firm known for their sensitivity to older buildings, provided a new staircase and entrance as well as an elevator and basic mechanical and electrical upgrades. Their solution repeated the shape of the spire and created a reduced and stylized version of the timber porch over the new doorway. At the top of this new stair the decorative half-timbering and tile-hanging has been preserved and offers a glimpse of the building as it was in 1882.

Music Hall was dedicated on October 3, 1882, with afternoon and evening concerts, including a Schumann Piano Concerto played by Professor Blodgett, the director of the Music School. After Sage Hall opened in 1924, the building was renamed in honor of Arthur Henry Pierce, who had been professor of psychology from 1900 to 1914. The department of psychology was housed in the building until 1966, when it moved to the Clark Science Center. Currently, Pierce Hall houses faculty offices and the Mary Maples Dunn conference room.

3. Lilly Hall *William C. Brockelsby, 1886*

Renovation *R. E. Dinneen Architects & Planners, 2002–03*

Lilly Hall was Smith's earliest science building and was touted as the "first building in the world erected for the teaching of science to women."[5] Housing the growing departments of botany, biology, physics, physiology, and chemistry, the building was a gift from A. T. Lilly, a wealthy silk manufacturer from Florence, Massachusetts, who also gave money for the Observatory (now demolished).

Lilly Hall was the first of six buildings designed for Smith College by William C. Brockelsby, who grew up and practiced in Hartford, Connecticut, after training in New York City in the offices of Richard Upjohn. Upjohn, best known for his Trinity Church in New York, was primarily an ecclesiastical architect and earned high praise for his work in the Gothic revival. After he returned to Conneticut, Brockelsby ran his own practice until the early twentieth century when he teamed up with H. H. Smith of Hartford. His practice was varied and included large commercial projects such as the National Fire Insurance Building in Hartford and several commissions for schools and churches in Connecticut and Massachusetts. In addition to his work at

Smith, for which he designed nine buildings between 1886 and 1900, he also designed the Forbes Library just across West Street from Lilly Hall.

Like Pierce Hall, Lilly is an interesting mix of utilitarian Gothic on the campus facade and a softer, more domestic style of architecture on what was considered at the time to be the main entrance of the building on West Street. Whereas the entrance from the campus side is highlighted by a simple, pedimented porch, the sheltering timber and stone porch over the entrance on West Street is much more welcoming. Twin gables to the left of the porch break out of the rectangular box while dormers and scalloped terra cotta moldings on the ridge enliven the roof. The contrast between the facades raises interesting questions about the public face of a women's college. College, Pierce, and Lilly halls do not look purely domestic, but all three have domestic features that soften their street facades and tie them stylistically to their residential neighbors.

As the sciences grew at Smith, Lilly proved too small to hold them all. Chemistry moved to Stoddard Hall in 1899. Geology moved out in 1910, and botany and biology followed in 1914. Physics remained the longest, and it was in Lilly Hall that the college installed a "Van de Graaff electrostatic generator, an 'atom smasher,' the first in a women's college and among the first in the initial development of nuclear physics."[6] Finally, in 1967 the physics department moved out and the School for Social Work took over along with the offices for graduate study. In the same year, the Lilly Pad Coffeehouse opened in the basement, planned and decorated by the 1967 sophomore class. The Afro-American Cultural Center, later renamed the Mwangi Cultural Center, replaced the Lilly Pad and took over the basement and first floor of Lilly Hall in 1968. Between 2002 and 2003 Lilly Hall underwent extensive renovations to upgrade the electrical and mechanical systems in the building and to make it accessible with an elevator and restrooms on every floor. The Mwangi Center relocated to new facilities in Davis Center in 2005. Despite its many interior changes and identities, the exterior of Lilly remains much as Brocklesby designed it in 1886.

4. Seelye Hall *York and Sawyer, 1899*

Renovations *Gillen Architects, 1994*

Plans for the construction of Seelye Hall began in 1898, when an anonymous donor gave the college $50,000 for an academic building, which was to be named after Smith's first president, L. Clark Seelye. After careful consideration, it was decided to place the new building, which provided much needed classrooms, faculty offices, and space for the growing library, behind College Hall, in the spot where Dewey House had been moved in 1875. Despite general outcry, Dewey was relocated again and Seelye Hall went up

Seelye Hall

with its curving back facing Lilly and Pierce halls and its main facade welcoming students from what is now called the Seelye Quad.

The emerging firm of York and Sawyer had previously designed Rockefeller Hall (1897) at Vassar College, which became the model for Seelye. Philip Sawyer and Edward Palmer York were working in the offices of McKim, Mead and White in New York City when they submitted plans for Vassar's academic building, which was based on a design for a high school by Sawyer and was a blend of Jacobian gables, dramatic quoins, and wonderfully heavy stacked stone columns.

While the overall layout and appearance of Seelye are the same as those of Rockefeller Hall, the main entrance is dramatized by a curving gable that juts into the roofline. Set within is a large curved window highlighted by a balcony. Heavy stone trim surrounds all three of the main doorways, banding the framing walls and the columns that flank the doors, while stone blocks and keystones crown the windows on the first two floors. The warm red brick and lively wall surface offset the solidity of the effusive stone trim, while the roofline culminates in a domed cupola in the style of Christopher Wren or Nicholas Hawksmoor.

Of the original design for a high school, Sawyer wrote that it had been planned as a "compact classroom building with its lowest story sunk to sill level to economize in height, its two ampitheaters superimposed in the rear, its classrooms each ideally lighted."[7] These two stacked amphitheaters became the library in Seelye Hall with radiating stacks accessed by curving stairs and balconies, study tables in the center, and enormous windows providing plenty of light. In 1909, with the erection of Neilson library, the Geology Department moved into this center space.

In 1993 William Gillen, a local architect from Amherst, was called in to discuss the addition of an elevator shaft to Seelye. A casual question about reaching the fourth floor, and the possibility for more faculty offices in this otherwise forgotten space, eventually led to an enormous renovation project.[8] Dormers were added to the fourth floor and twelve new faculty offices were gained. The basement became a state-of-the-art computer lab. What had once been a two-story library space was divided in two, providing a much-needed faculty lounge on the second floor and the Jacobson Center for Writing, Teaching and Learning on the third. The Jacobson Center space saw the most dramatic changes. The great height of the room made it possible to enlarge the balcony and small offices could be added on both floors. The result of the ten-month renovation project was what the architect had hoped for—an "invisible" architecture that brought the building into the twenty-first century without changing its dramatic early-twentieth-century facade.[9]

5. Hubbard House   *Peabody & Stearns, 1879*

Dining room addition   *David P. Handlin and Associates, 1993*

Renovations   *Alderman & MacNeish, 1994*

Hubbard House was the third cottage Peabody & Stearns designed for the college within a three-year period and thus stands as testimony to the rapid success and growth of Smith in its early years. It was named in honor of Sophia Smith's close advisor, George Warner Hubbard. The original floor plans by Peabody & Stearns reveal a great deal about life inside the Smith cottage. Visitors and students entered first a reception room, which, in turn, offered access to the living room, the matron's rooms, and a corridor that ran through the building. The dining room faced west, just opposite the living room, and at the end of the corridor were rooms for a member of faculty and student bedrooms, called "studies" on the original plans. On the second and third floors studies of different sizes branched off the central corridor with toilets and baths at the north end. The fourth floor held storage space and the maids' rooms, all reached by the smaller back stair. While obviously designed to accommodate many residents under one roof, the basic ingredients of the domestic house are all included. On the plans, there is a note that above each study door there should be a "light." These windows ensured that while students had the relative privacy of their own room, the matron could easily enforce President Seelye's strict 10 p.m. bedtime rule. Any lights still on after 10 p.m. could be spotted by walking down the corridor, and the student would be reminded to stop studying or

Hubbard House

socializing and go to sleep. This rule was part of the overall concern at Smith, as at all women's colleges, to protect students' health by ensuring that they got plenty of rest.

The exterior of Hubbard, reminiscent of Girton College's Old Hall (1972), is sheathed in simple red brick. This is elaborated in the paired gables at each end of the building, where a stepped brick pattern provides decorative relief and painted barge boards add a sheltering touch. The main entrance is under a timber porch, which runs between the gabled ends. Other domestic details include two small, rectangular dormers that frame a large shed dormer, a pattern that is repeated on the floor above with smaller windows. The gables and dormers of the front facade are also found on the back, where an enlarged dining room now extends out past the gable ends and fills the middle space. This addition of 1993, by David P. Handlin and Associates, is part of a new scheme at Smith to consolidate the dining facilities on campus. The extension is sensitively rendered, respecting the scale of the house and borrowing the curving brackets of the front porch as details on both the exterior and interior of the dining room.

For many Smith alumnae, the house they lived in remains an important part of their memories of college life. A small pamphlet from 1959, entitled "Welcome to Hubbard House," by Eloise, and given to new students, offers a record of life in Hubbard. Eloise, the wealthy character made famous in books by Kay Thompson, details what the new student can expect to find when she enters Hubbard on her first day:

Going into Hubbard you will immediately feel at home because of the general atmosphere of the house, but mostly because of our house mother who will bustle out to rescue you with the inimitable warmth and enthusiasm she shows for each one of her girls. . . . To your right you will see a nice home-like room. This is Mrs. Shulte's sitting room where you relax and chat after dinner over a demi-tasse. . . . To your left is the living room which is rawther [sic] well lived in. The piano being played frequently, a gab session about books, boys or bridge always going, a fire burning in the winter, and, in general, agreeable chaos.[10]

6. Washburn House   *Peabody & Stearns, 1878*

Washburn House was the second dormitory that Peabody & Stearns built for Smith College. It was named for William Barrett Washburn, who served the college as one of the original trustees appointed by Sophia Smith. He was also governor of Massachusetts between 1872 and 1874, United States Senator from 1874 to 1875, and a trustee of his alma mater, Yale University, from 1869 to 1881. His two daughters each spent two years at Smith.

After its opening, Washburn House soon became famous for its Saturday night dramatic productions, which ranged from one-acts and burlesques to more serious plays and evolved into the dramatic club Olla Podrida. In the Depression years between 1932 and 1938 the dormitory was used as a cooperative house to help students financially. After 1938 it became the Spanish House, where Spanish-language meals and weekly teas in Spanish took place, offering a brief cultural experience to women who wished to go to Spain for their Junior Year Abroad but were unable to because of the Spanish Civil War. In 1943 Washburn was modestly remodelled along the Spanish theme, with prints of famous Spanish paintings lining the walls and with a fireplace that was tiled in yellow and blue tiles from southern Spain.

By 1955 a dearth of interested students ended Washburn's career as the Spanish House on campus and it became an ordinary residence. Yet in a student handbook from 1961 some rooms are still referred to by their Spanish names. For instance, the "Salita" or sitting room was the domain of the housemother and available for entertaining with her permission. The "Fumidor" was the common study room, which contained the library, where smoking was allowed.[11]

The plan of Washburn is a departure from that seen in Peabody & Stearn's first residence for Smith, Hatfield House. For Washburn, Peabody & Stearns used a simple shallow H-plan, with gabled ends pulled out from the central core. This scheme was later repeated at Hubbard House and in future residences by Brockelsby. At Washburn, the entrance is placed at

TOP: *Washburn House*
BOTTOM: *Neilson Library*

the far right end of the central block and is marked by a welcoming timber porch.

As with Smith's other early cottages the exterior is clad in simple red brick, marked by narrow bands of decorative brickwork above the second- and third-floor windows. A central dormer, flanked by gabled dormers that are decorated by board-and-batten timberwork, provides light for the third-story rooms. Most unusual is the way these dormers are cut through the center by chimneys. This treatment is also found on Hubbard and Hatfield houses and was particular to Peabody & Stearns' work on campus. All the windows were originally framed by shutters, which added to the residential appearance of the dormitory.

7. Neilson Library   *Lord and Hewlett, 1909*

Addition   *Karl S. Putnam, 1938*

Addition   *O'Connor and Kilham, 1962*

Addition   *Cambridge Seven Associates, 1975*

Renovations   *Juster Pope Frazier, 1998*

For the first thirty years of its existence, Smith College had no library of its own. Space was made in College Hall and later in Seelye Hall for the college's growing collection, and for many years the college paid a minimum fee to the Forbes Library, just across West Street, for the use of its books. When the Forbes Library raised its fees for Smith students, the voices calling for an independent library grew louder, and a Library Committee was formed to study the needs of the college.

By 1908 the college had accepted plans for a library by the architects Lord and Hewlett of New York. Austin W. Lord had studied in Rome and worked in the offices of McKim, Mead and White until 1894; his partner, James M. Hewlett, studied at Columbia and at the Ecole des Beaux Arts in Paris. In light of the architects' classical education, the plans for the new library are hardly surprising. The building presents a restrained and balanced Renaisssance design, which looks to McKim, Mead and White's Boston Public Libary of 1888. The brick, together with the red sandstone details around the windows and doors, Connecticut granite columns framing the entries, and the eight rondeles that divide the first floor from the second, combine to present an understated, classical elegance.

The architects drew up the plans in the full knowledge that expansion would be required in the future. The entrance front and back side formed the long sides of an H, connected through the center by a narrower section for stacks. The browsing room is the only original interior that remains. Though often lined with chairs for lectures, it still resembles the description given in 1909 in the *Boston Transcript*. The author praises the room, pointing out that it is "equipped like a private library. On the floor is a large rug. The open fireplace, the easy chairs and small tables, the open shelves with volumes roughly classified into poetry, music, essays, fiction, and the like, the table for new books, all make this result."[12]

The members of the Library Committee were prescient when they stipulated that the library should be easily added onto. By 1937 Karl S. Putnam, an architect who taught at Smith for many years and had worked with Ames and Dodge on some of the early buildings in the Quad, drew up plans for an expansion to the north of the front entrance. This filled in the first side of the H. The inclusion of 107 carrels was significant as part of a wider movement at Smith toward more independent study. In the past students had been assigned the same books to read in class. By 1937 greater emphasis was paid to individual Honors work. Thus many duplicate volumes were no longer necessary, and large reading rooms were broken up by carrels for private study. Putnam's addition picked up the red sandstone used in the details of the orginal library and stretched it in long vertical panels along the facade. Between these panels are large sash windows framed in black. The smooth clean lines of the sandstone and the lack of ornament reflect a move in the late 1930s toward the modern style of architecture. The architectural simplicity of Putnam's addition does little to detract from its older neighbor.

The growth of the library continued. In 1959 the new president, Thomas Mendenhall, hired the firm of O'Connor and Kilham of New York, who had recently completed carefully worked out libraries for Princeton University and Trinity College, Hartford, to design another extension. The facade facing Burton Hall is the only part of O'Connor and Kilham's work that is still visible. As with Putnam's addition, the architects used long vertical slabs of reddish sandstone, which are suspended out from the wall surface allowing only filtered light through the windows. The actual walls of the building are of red brick. O'Connor and Kilham also renovated the interiors, thoroughly modernizing the stacks.

In 1974 Cambridge Seven Associates, a firm famous for the design of the New England Aquarium in Boston, enlarged and redesigned the library yet again. Their early plans extended the building dramatically to the south and included the demolition of Alumnae Gymnasium. This raised a great and lengthy protest from alumnae and some faculty and delayed the expansion of the library for four years. By 1976, under Jill Ker Conway's presidency, it was agreed to include the gym in the overall scheme. Cambridge Seven Associates enveloped most of the 1962 addition to the north and all of O'Connor and Kilham's work to the south. They abandoned the red sandstone of the first two additions and opted for simple red brick walls with windows that are set deep within the walls, a means of sheltering the interiors from too much direct sunlight.

The extension is linked to Wright Hall via a bridge on the second floor of the library. To the south, an underpass was included to maintain access from the front quadrangle to the east and the Science Quad to the west. A small glassed-in bridge connects the library with Alumnae Gym, which now holds the college archives and the Center for Media Production. The interiors were once again renovated to include many small study rooms, seminar spaces, and more stacks. The entire length of the building, now almost four hundred feet long, is uninterrupted on the upper floors.

In 1998 the firm of Juster Pope Frazier renovated the entryway and circulation desk as well as the Mortimer Rare Book Room now housed on the third floor. By adding modest quantities of dark wood paneling, their renovations served to soften the stark modernism of the 1970s and bring echoes of the original building back into these public spaces.

8. Alumnae Gymnasium *William C. Brockelsby, 1891*

Addition *William C. Brockelsby, 1892*

Renovations *Cambridge Seven Associates, 1982*

Alumnae Gymnasium was Brockelsby's fourth building for Smith College. From its earliest days Smith had included instruction in physical education as an important means of maintaining women's health and strength while at college. The instructor of gymnastics, Miss Gertrude Walker, pleaded for a gymnasium to meet the needs of her students and to keep up with Vassar College and Bryn Mawr, whose new gyms were state of the art. In 1888 the alumnae began raising funds and by 1890 were able to contribute $23,000 toward the total cost of $30,000.

Brockelsby's largest building for Smith is a wonderful combination of Queen Anne massing and details with a Richardsonian stability. Great rough-hewn sandstone stringcourses and an arch over the main window are offset by the delicate terra-cotta swag in the central panel, the scalloped roofline, and the gentle curve of the slender flèche. The original entrances are paired on either end of the building, highlighted by timber porches. By 1892 a small wing was added to the south, which introduced the Flemish stepped gable to the campus and a Palladian window. Both features are typical of the Queen Anne style, which was very popular in the 1870s and

OPPOSITE: *Alumnae Gymnasium*

Alumnae Gymnasium, interior

1880s, especially for domestic architecture. Characteristic of the style are curving or stepped gables, classical details such as swags, pediments, columns, and pilasters, as well as a picturesque asymmetry. The Queen Anne was a hybrid that did not strive for the formal grandeur of the classical tradition and was free of the religious associations of the Gothic revival.

In its heyday, the gymnasium was home to the first women's basketball match in 1893, a game introduced by the first director of the gym, Senda Berenson. But by the 1960s the building was no longer in use, and ideas about its re-use were discussed. One student recomended converting it to a spartan lodging for men visiting girlfriends on campus.[13] In 1974, as plans progressed to enlarge Neilson Library, Alumnae Gym was slated for demolition. This move prompted a swift and vocal outcry among alumnae and faculty, who saw the architectural value and beauty of the old gym. The debate was long and challenging. President Thomas Mendenhall argued that older buildings had already been saved and that to renovate Alumnae Gym would cost more money than it was worth and would not go far in providing the much needed space for the library. While the trustees and administration went ahead with demolition plans, a Committee to Preserve Alumnae Gym formed in 1975, led by William L. MacDonald, the Alice Pratt Brown Professor of Art.

The committee had several members who were active in the burgeoning field of historic preservation and managed to get Brockelsby's building listed in the National Register of Historic Places. They applied for, and received, a small grant from the National Trust for Historic Preservation for a feasibility study to look into possible re-use of the building, undertaken by architect Harry Weese.

While Weese presented a plan, the trustees eventually agreed to go back to a much earlier plan submitted by Cambridge Seven Associates, which would save and integrate the older building into Neilson Library. By 1977 Alumnae Gym had been preserved. While making much needed structural improvements, the architects left the wonderful wooden trusses in the roof exposed as well as the brick walls at either end of the building. The large windows, which used to illuminate women's gymnastics classes, now generously light oak tables at which scholars of women's history sit and

read. The western side is lined with offices, whose glass walls maintain the
open airiness of the interior. The ground floor now houses the library's
media center, while the second floor holds the archival stacks.

9. Wright Hall   *William and Geoffrey Platt, 1961*

Wright Hall was Smith's third purely academic building. By the mid-twentieth
century, Seelye Hall could no longer provide all the classroom and office
space for the college. While room was found in Neilson for the overflow, this
was not a satisfactory solution and as early as 1957 President Benjamin
Wright began working with the architects William and Geoffrey Platt of New
York on plans for a new academic building. Plans by the landscape architect
John Nolan dating from 1915 included an academic quadrangle, which
suggested the siting of Wright Hall opposite Seelye Hall on the site of
Wallace House, which was to be moved to another location.

However, the lack of funds together with disagreements among the
architects, Board of Trustees, and certain faculty members meant that the
planning of the new building proceeded only slowly. By 1959 President
Wright had resigned and was replaced by Mendenhall. When the relocation
of Wallace House proved to be more expensive than first thought, the building was razed. Once Mendenhall saw the site without Wallace House, he was
determined to keep that space open, arguing that, "Dewey now comes into
all its glory and the sense of an inner campus, with light, space and trees
is greatly increased."[14] Thus the current location of Wright Hall in close
proximity to the library was chosen (at the expense of the old observatory).
The Platt brothers' original plans for a brick neo-classical building in keeping
with their previous work on campus were also abandoned, in favor of a
more modern design, reflecting a growing tendency in campus buildings to
follow current trends in architecture.

Wright Hall did fill a desperate need, creating seventy new offices
for faculty, a state-of-the-art language laboratory, a social science lab, small
seminar rooms, a lounge, and a large lecture hall. It was built in a T-shape,
with the long arms of the T holding the offices and large lecture hall and the
shorter trunk housing more offices and the lounge. Upon the completion of
the 1962 addition to Neilson Library, Wright was connected via a bridge to
the library.

The main entrance to Wright Hall is to the north of the library. The
building differs dramatically from its neighbors, with a great facade of glass
divided vertically by two-story cement arcades that envelop the building and
unify it. Between the arcades the glass facade is delineated by steel frames
that separate the clear glass windows from the decorative opaque panels
dividing the first floor from the second. The arms of the T, longer to the west

than the east, consist of a series of bays articulated by the cement arcades and filled in with red brick. Again, metal-frame windows punctuate the surface. A squat square tower sits above the center junction. Decorative abstract cement panels, almost lacy in their appearance, envelop this small block.

The use of these open-work cement blocks looks to Frank Lloyd Wright and his work in California in the 1920s and was new both to the campus and to the work of the Platt brothers. A stone terrace on the north of the building offers a gathering place outdoors for students and faculty, while to the south, the basement floor is accessible via a narrower stone terrace. Though Wright Hall is dramatically different in style from its academic predecessor, Seelye, it shares with the earlier building an emphatic use of contrasting materials that add vigor to the campus.

10. Hatfield Hall *Peabody & Stearns, 1876*

Addition *Peabody & Stearns, 1894*

Addition *Goody Clancy Architects, 1996*

Originally called Hatfield House, this was the first purpose-built cottage on campus. It was also the first purpose-built house for a women's college in the United States. Smith was begun a few years after Vassar and Wellesley, and this delay gave the original trustees a chance to learn from the other schools and to adopt or reject various aspects of their organization. Revolutionary in the planning of Smith was the rejection of the all-inclusive grand building that housed students, classrooms, faculty, and the dining room. Large institutional buildings such as those at Wellesley and Vassar were designed like the nineteenth-century asylum and prison, for supervision and containment. But Seelye and his collegues argued for a smaller, more domestic setting for their college as a way to protect women's feminine natures. As Helen Lefkowitz Horowitz writes:

> Womanliness for him, as for John Greene, meant that students remained within the culture of the family and the town.... Educate women in college but keep them symbolically at home. Erect a central college building for instruction and surround it with cottages where students live in familial settings. Keep them in daily contact with men as president and faculty.[15]

The domestic environment was considered a safeguard for women as they left home for an academic education. Other women's colleges such as Bryn Mawr and later Wellesley adopted the cottage example for many years.

Hatfield was built as a somewhat typical house, with a parlor, kitchen, dining room, and pantry on the first floor and twenty-three

TOP: *Wright Hall*
BOTTOM: *Hatfield Hall*

bedrooms on the second and third floors. The resident faculty member and the house matron also had rooms in the house. Hatfield was originally placed behind the newly moved Dewey House and was relocated in 1908 to its present site to make room for the new library. Like the cottages that followed, Hatfield had a long porch that extended along the south side of the house. Characteristic of Peabody & Stearns' work at Smith, the dormers in the third floor are divided by chimneys, which are framed on each side by windows and break through the dormer's roofline. A bay window beside the entrance and a new gabled wing that extended to the north were added in 1894. These additions are thought to be by Peabody & Stearns as well, as they blend harmoniously with the older building, continuing the simple red brick and the barge-board pattern framing the gables.

By 1926 the college could no longer afford to run Hatfield as a residence. Its relatively small size meant that it never fully supported itself financially, so it was converted into a hall with classrooms and faculty offices. To mark the change, Mary Breese Fuller (class of 1894) wrote about her memories of Hatfield House under the lively and stimulating tutelage of Miss Mary Augusta Jordan, professor of English and rhetoric. As the resident faculty member in Hatfield, she filled the house with guests such as Henry James, Mark Twain, and Charles Dudly Warner. Fuller remembered that "The antics of Mr. Clemens, . . . which led Mrs. Aldrich [the House Matron] to refuse him a seat at her dinner table, were joyfully welcomed by us."[16]

In 1996 the firm Goody Clancy, who had previously worked on Pierce Hall, renovated Hatfield, designing a new stair tower and elevator shaft for the house. Both were inserted on the east front, subtly filling in a corner where the addition of 1894 met the original house. They also added a glazed entrance porch and upgraded the heating, electrical, mechanical, and plumbing components while replacing the slate roofs and copperwork and cleaning the masonry. Though Hatfield Hall has undergone many changes over the years, the small timbered porch at the entrance leads the visitor to the old staircase and the original oak newel posts over which countless students have passed their hands on their way to meals, lectures, or Friday afternoon tea.

11. Dewey Hall (originally Dewey House)

Thomas Pratt, 1826–27

Addition *architect unknown, 1898*

Renovations *Dietz & Company, 1994*

Dewey Hall has always been an important part of Smith College. The trustees bought it in 1871 before the college had become a reality. The building originally stood facing Elm Street just beside the Lyman Estate, where College Hall would be placed. It was moved in 1875 behind College Hall, where Seelye now stands. While the founders were intent on keeping their students involved in the life of the town, attending local churches and using the local library, their decision to move Dewey away from a public road to a more private area suggests that Seelye and others wanted the first college residence to be more secluded and protected. Gateway, the first president's house, was built where Dewey had been.

This protective domesticity can also be seen in the structure of life in Dewey House in its early days. House matron Elizabeth J. Hopkins looked after the students, attending to the daily routine of managing servants, keeping the house accounts, and purchasing supplies. President Seelye remembered her as "a good housekeeper; a woman familiar with the best social usages; and … a winsome personality. She soon succeeded in organizing the household as a private family in which she took the position of 'house mother.'"[17] In this early experiment in women's higher education, the appearance of accepted modes of domesticity and feminine behavior was vital.

Dewey was built in 1827 as a private home for Judge Charles A. Dewey by the local builder Thomas Pratt. Dewey was an important figure in Northampton during the first half of the nineteenth century, serving in the House of Representatives and in the Senate in the 1820s and 1830s. He built his house in the popular Greek revival style, which Ithiel Town had brought to Northampton in his Bower House of 1827. The Greek revival was increasingly favored for its stylistic simplicity and elegance and for its associations with early Greek democracy.

Dewey's famous white facade with its calm symmetry and graceful Ionic columns supporting a simple pediment stands out on a campus otherwise dominated by busier Victorian and twentieth-century buildings of red brick. The interior originally consisted of front and back parlors, rooms for Mrs. Hopkins on the first floor, and students' bedrooms on the second. In 1898, when Dewey was moved to its present location to make way for Seelye Hall, an ell was added to the back of the house. It was clad in the traditional clapboard of New England and included twin gables separated by small dormers in the roof. This addition provided a much larger dining room on the first floor and more bedrooms on the second and new third

floors. A beautifully curving staircase, recorded in many old photographs, connected the first and second floors.

Dewey maintained its residential status for many years. In 1991, the college decided that its domestic days were over. It had been housing Ada Comstock students for a long time, but there were not enough on-campus residents to fill the house. Thus the Adas relocated to 150 Elm Street, and Dewey was converted into faculty offices and small lecture rooms. Ann Burger, Dean of the College at the time, praised the changes and noted that Dewey Hall "will provide the entire campus with access to one of our oldest buildings."[18]

Walking through Dewey today, one can catch a glimpse of its former glory. The back parlor survives as a meeting room and visitors can enjoy the original mantlepiece. Over the doors and windows the beautiful moldings remain, fluted with foliated squares at each corner—elaborate details from an earlier time.

12. Clark Hall (originally Dewey Annex)

Peabody & Stearns, 1878

One of the most lucrative and busy aspects of the firm of Peabody & Stearns was the design of summer homes for the wealthy. In places like Lenox and Stockbridge, Massachusetts, or Newport, Rhode Island, the practice left its mark with such estates. Clark House, No. 50 Elm Street, was an early summer cottage by the architects. The Clark family, after whom the house is named, was a very old and established family in Northampton. In 1878

ABOVE: *Clark Hall*
OPPOSITE: *Dewey Hall*

Charles H. Clark, who lived and worked in New York City, hired Peabody & Stearns to design a summer house for him where an earlier family house had been. It is interesting that Clark decided to rebuild on land so close to an emerging women's college, but perhaps in 1878 he did not imagine that the college would grow as it did.

Clark was one of the many houses the college acquired as it grew. Purchased in 1889 as an investment, Smith remodeled the house so it could accommodate more students and leased it to landlords from the town who ran it as a boarding house. In 1908 the college took control of the house and opened it as a residence. Clark House is typical of the popular shingle style of the 1870s and 1880s, so called for its reliance on large gables with shingle infill, and characteristic of the more modest homes that Peabody & Stearns designed. The exterior is clad in clapboard on the lower half and shingles on the upper floors and gables. The great front gable is stepped and shingled with a Palladian window and curving window aprons, characteristic of the Queen Anne style. Old photographs in the college archives show that the upper shingles were originally stained or painted a darker color than the lower clapboards. It is now painted a warm beige with the trim and details highlighted in white. Presently known as Clark Hall, it houses administrative offices.

13. Brown Fine Arts Center *John Andrews, 1972*

Renovations and addition *Polshek Partnership, 2000–02*

Smith College has always been strongly committed to the study of the fine arts. When College Hall first opened, plaster casts and prints were displayed in the attic space for study purposes. The college was in the process of raising money for more adequate gallery space when a Northampton businessman, Winthrop Hillyer, surprised everyone by donating $25,000 for an art building. The original building, designed by Peabody & Stearns in their signature red brick high Victorian style with touches of Queen Anne, opened in 1882.

In 1910 Christine A. Graham, a senior at Smith, made a gift of $27,500 for an addition to the Hillyer building. This extension, called Graham Hall, provided space for a large lecture room, more exhibition space, and studios. Built of red brick in a similar style, it blended well with the original Peabody & Stearns building. In 1926 Smith professor Dwight William Tryon and his wife Alice gave money for the art department and the museum to separate into two relatively independent units. The Tryon Art Gallery, designed by Frederick L. Ackerman, presented a symmetrical facade with classical arches and details in light red brick and marble trim.

Brown Fine Arts Center

By the late 1960s these three buildings were not meeting the art department's needs, and despite the protests of a small minority of preservationists and professors who asked that the buildings be saved, the Board of Trustees and Mendenhall decided to raze all three as well as Gateway. John Andrews, an Australian architect who practiced in Canada, was commissioned for the new building. At the time, Andrews was receiving great acclaim for his work on Harvard's Gund Hall, designed in the Brutalist style, so called for its reliance on great expanses of reinforced concrete, often with the bolts left showing and the veins of the building (the pipes and ductwork) also exposed. At Smith the architect made modest efforts to unite the art center with its older neighbors, but on the whole his design made an aggressive statement about modern materials and construction techniques.

By 1995, when these modern materials and techniques had begun to fail and the building needed numerous repairs and dramatic upgrades, the college began a study to assess the changing needs of the art department and museum, the demands of new technologies, and the viability of the existing (and not very popular) building. The college did not want to raze the Andrews building, as it had worked fairly well in its overall plan and as a connector between the residences east of Elm Street and the academic hub of the campus. The Polshek Partnership won the commission for the new art center because the New York firm was willing to work with the skeletal remains of the Andrews building and to integrate the varied aspects of the art complex within the basic footprint.[19]

Polshek Partnership's design consciously re-introduced the red brick of so many campus buildings and in certain areas laid the brick in decorative patterns to tie it further to existing buildings. They glazed in the central courtyard, which plays a pivitol role linking the campus and the

LEFT: *Brown Fine Arts Center*, Liquid Origins, Fluid Dreams, *designed by Sandy Skoglund*
RIGHT: *Brown Fine Arts Center*, Catching the Drift, *designed by Ellen Driscoll*

street as well as the museum with the art department and library. The museum, which stands to the north, is visually linked to the new building by a tall glass wall, which looks down into the central courtyard. Large expanses of glass continue around the building, covered by aluminum screens to filter the light on the inside and soften the glare on the exterior. The stair towers, defined by the earlier building, remain and have been clad in a gray zinc, giving them the sort of definition that Victorians would have loved—interior spaces easily identifiable by exterior features.

James Polshek and Susan Rodriguez wrote that this project "validates our belief that respect for an institution's history and context can be reinforced by an architecture of our time."[20] This airy, light-filled building in which the different elements overlap and complement each other realizes the architects' ambitions. The unity of function and form can be seen on a grand scale in the overall design and use of materials. It is also evident on a more intimate level. When visiting the museum and its important collection, visitors should make sure to see the washrooms in the basement level. Designed by the artists Ellen Driscoll (women's washroom, called *Catching the Drift*) and Sandy Skoglund (men's washroom, called *Liquid Origins, Fluid Dreams*), the tiles, sinks, and toilets unite to make surprising and whimsical spaces.

OPPOSITE: *Brown Fine Arts Center, interior*

Lawrence House

14. Lawrence and Morris Houses   *William C. Brockelsby, 1891*

Lawrence and Morris houses, both named for alumnae, were built in 1891 to fill the college's urgent need for more accommodation for its growing number of students. Lawrence House's namesake was Elizabeth Crocker Lawrence from the class of 1883. She returned to Smith for a master's degree in 1889, served as a trustee from 1894 to 1900, and was the president of the Alumnae Association between 1909 and 1911. Morris is named for Kate Eugenia Morris from the class of 1879, who pursued a Ph.D. at Smith in 1882 and was the first alumna to sit on the Board of Trustees.

Lawrence became a cooperative house in 1912, offering reduced tuition and board to students of limited financial means, who were in turn required to perform various chores such as dish washing, sweeping, serving meals, and keeping rooms clean. An article in the *Girls' Companion* from 1913 described the nature of the residents' work:

> All of the work is thoroughly systematized, each squad of workers having a chairman who carefully directs the work so that it may run along without friction and as expeditiously as possible. It is worth a good deal to the girls to learn how to do work in this way. One thing is insisted upon, and that is absolute thoroughness.... The principles of doing housework on a scientific plan are here carried out as far as possible.[1]

This scientific approach to housework was part of a larger move-ment in Great Britain and the U.S., where domestic hygiene was included in the curricula of women's colleges: at Smith it was taught in the physical education department. While they would seem out of place in the twenty-first century, such courses were at the time considered an important part of a woman's overall education and beneficial to the overall health of the nation. Using scientific phraseology lent domestic chores an importance few today would feel they deserve.

As a cooperative, Lawrence was a very popular place to live. Even women who did not need financial assistance applied for rooms, and resi-dents took great pride in their domestic efficiency.

Unlike Lawrence, Morris House remained an ordinary residence on campus. Many dramatic performances were produced here and two notable early alumnae were among its residents: Florence Homer Snow (class of 1904), who organized the Alumnae Association, and Edith Hill (class of 1903), who began a newsletter with other alumnae that became the *Smith Alumnae Quarterly* in 1910. While domestic science became identified with Lawrence House, the domestic nature of Smith's student residences has been alive and well in Morris. A *New Student's Handbook* of 1987 reassures freshmen:

> Because Morris is a HOUSE, we try to make it a HOME. Everyone living
> there is like a family. We hope that you will grow to become as fond of
> our house as we are and that you will consider it as your home and all
> of us like family.[2]

Originally, Lawrence and Morris appeared more domestic than their current exteriors suggest. The houses consist of long rectangular blocks, which are broken up by gabled ends and a central gambreled gable. These were once enlivened with details borrowed from the stick and Queen Anne styles of domestic architecture popular at the time. Painted shutters framed every window, and the gables were softened by decorative barge-boards. Wavy clapboards decorated the pediment over the porch and the smaller dormers in the roof. Such details have now disappeared, but the sheltering porches and bay windows beside the entrances provide echoes of the original design. The twin houses are still graceful residences, their warm brick walls interupted by rough-hewn sandstone window lintels and stringcourses. As a result of the dining conversions of the 1990s, when the kitchens and dining rooms of the two houses were closed, residents now eat in Tyler House and enjoy enlarged studies and lounge spaces on the ground floors of Morris and Lawrence.

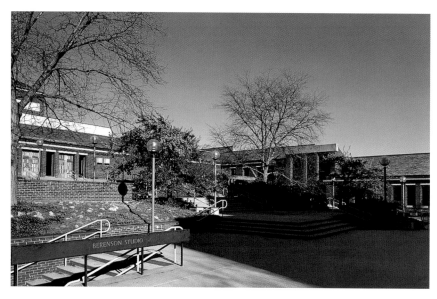

Mendenhall Center

15. Mendenhall Center for the Performing Arts

Westermann Miller and Associates, 1968

Renovations *Perkins Eastman Architects, 2003*

Under the presidency of Mendenhall, the campus underwent major changes. With his enthusiasm and energy, huge building campaigns were taken on to house the sciences, arts, physical education, and the performing arts. The building that took the longest to complete, from the nascent idea to its opening, was the Mendenhall Center for the Performing Arts. As early as 1961, Mendenhall began correspondence about building a theater, seeking advice from colleagues and experts in the field. As the needs of the theater department solidified, Mendenhall started working together with Helge Westermann of Westermann Miller and Associates, who had just completed work for the Julliard School of Music at Lincoln Center and came highly recommended by the dean, Mark Schubart.

Correspondence between the architect and the college was long and sometimes tiresome. When the trustees, Mendenhall, and the theater department finally agreed on a program, the building needed to house five separate but related elements: a 450-seat theater, a music library, a dance studio, and an experimental theater as well as backstage elements such as a shop room, green room, dressing rooms, and space for props and scenery.

OPPOSITE: *Mendenhall Center, interior*

TOP: *Scott Gymnasium, Olin Fitness Center, and Ainsworth Gymnasium (from left to right)*
BOTTOM: *Ainsworth Gymnasium*

Early on the college decided to build near Sage Hall so that the Department of Music could be closely connected to the theater. The main theater (Theater 14) is directly opposite Sage Hall, with two arms extending out toward Sage and enclosing a courtyard. A geometric maze of brick steps and patios framed by smooth cement and medium-sized boulders, the courtyard complements the irregular and assymmetrical massing of the various elements of the building. Westermann favored greater use of cast concrete for the building, but Mendenhall was skeptical, arguing that "cast concrete, unless it is treated in a very expensive fashion as was done in the new college at Yale, tends to weather rather poorly and to become rather dirty and unattractive all too soon."[3] Instead, brick was once again the material of choice, tying the new center to its neighbors. Thus Mendenhall rejected the Brutalist stlye of Louis Kahn and Paul Rudolph at Yale in favor of the Scandanavian tradition of modern architecture as seen in the work of Alvar Aalto. The contrasting use of brick and concrete and the powerful use of geometric forms come from Aalto's influence.

Similarly, on the interior, warm golden oak trim highlights the geometric forms and helps to define spaces. Brick also lines the walls where the jagged, irregular bricks add noticeable texture and the brownish shade is offset by soft gray concrete and honey-colored oak. Long banks of clerestory windows provide light as do vertical floor-to-ceiling glass panes that are interspersed between the walls. Overall, the effects of indirect light and volumes that open out into other spaces make for complicated, exciting interior spaces.

16. Ainsworth/Scott Gymnasium Complex

Scott Gymnaisum *Ames and Dodge, 1924*

Ainsworth Gymnasium, addition and renovation *The Architects' Collaborative, 1973*

Indoor Track and Tennis Facility *The Architects' Collaborative, 1986*

Olin Fitness Center, addition and renovation *Leers Weinzapfel Associates, 2003*

The history of Scott Gymnasium and its later additions and renovations in many ways highlights the history of physical education for women at college. Early leaders in women's education considered a rigorous and disciplined program of exercise to be of vital importance. They believed that without plenty of rest and exercise female students would be prone to overworking themselves academically. Recognizing this concern for women's health, Seelye was quick to build a simple wooden structure where Lilly Hall now stands for the required gymnastics classes. In 1891 Alumnae Gym replaced this temporary structure, providing students with a chance to swim as well as carry out their gymnastics routine.

By the early 1920s it was clear that Alumnae Gym was no longer adequate. The popular basketball games were overcrowded and the pool (only twenty by twelve feet) was painfully small. Indeed, an article from the time promised that "No longer after 1924, will Smith College mermaids have to suffer dizziness from swimming madly around."[4] By 1922 President Neilson had begun corrresponding with the architects Ames and Dodge, who were already working at Smith on the early houses of the Quadrangle, about building a new gymnasium. Named for, and partly funded by, Colonel Walter Scott of New York City, the resulting gymnasium continued the neo-classicism of Sage Hall and the Quadrangle. Classical details include the simple doric columns that flank the entrance, a fan-light above the door with a Roman urn, and two arched niches beside the door holding iron lamps. The volume of the interior space is articulated by a large gable roof, which is echoed by the gable of the porch. White-trimmed sash windows light the interior. A rectangular extension with large, arched windows was sited further down the hillside to the west and housed the pool. Its flat roof served as a terrace in summer.

The new building made possible changes in physical education that lasted for many years. As the local *Springfield Sunday Republican* remarked, it

> ushered in several changes in the curriculum of the department of physical education. Some of the innovations are the permission to substitute two hours of swimming a week for formal gymnastics if approved by the department; the ruling that hockey shall be a fall sport, and that basketball a winter one; and the introduction of soccer to replace cricket.[5]

But by the early 1970s complaints similar to those heard fifty years earlier were being voiced. The Smith press reported that the Scott Gym was woefully inadequate for the needs of students. Piper Wentz wrote in the *Sophian*:

> Scott gym was rated "fair" by the Committee. Undersized courts for basketball, badminton and volleyball; poor lighting; and poor temperature control were the reasons given. The swimming pool, virtually a three-lane sink, fared worse.[6]

The result of such criticism was the addition of Ainsworth Gym, named for alumna and Director of Physical Education Dorothy S. Ainsworth. Designed by the Architects' Collaborative (TAC), the addition was yet another of Mendenhall's building projects. In keeping with his taste for contemporary design, it is an addition that acknowledges its neighbors in the use of red brick and simple geometric volumes, but otherwise boldly asserts its modernity.

The old swimming pool is a key element in the addition. Rather than tear it down, the architects, led by David G. Sheffield, appreciated the elegance of its vaulted ceiling and decided to fill in the pool and make the space a students' lounge. With open balconies looking down into the lounge, this area acts as an integral part of the circulation, blending the old and new buildings. In the tradition of the Pompidou Center in Paris (Renzo Piano and Richard Rogers, 1974), or the Science Center at Wellesley College (Charles F. Rogers II, 1975), duct work and piping were left exposed and painted in bold colors, emphasizing the industrial functions of the building.

While TAC's work brought Smith's facilities up to date in the 1970s, by the year 2003 the gymnasium complex needed yet another extension. The firm of Leers Weinzapfel and Associates, of Boston, designed an addition that increased the connection between the two older structures. Called the Olin Fitness Center, this glass envelope sits snugly between Scott and Ainsworth and adds seven thousand square feet of space for exercise and fitness, housing treadmills, weights, stairclimbers, TVs, a new stretching area, and a service desk. The center is thoroughly contemporary, with its glazed membrane stretching between the two older buildings. Yet it honors the historic fabric leaving brick walls exposed and opening up dramatic vistas into different levels. In a sense this new area, with its emphasis on personal fitness, marks a return to Smith's early gymnastics classes when a woman's health was considered a vital ingredient to her academic success at college.

17. Sage Hall *Delano and Aldrich, 1924*

Renovations *Polshek Partnership Architects, 1991*

In the 1920s, during William Allan Neilson's presidency, Smith College began to expand beyond its original footprint. The Quadrangle pushed the boundaries to the north, while Sage Hall was the first college building to cross Green Street to the south. Planned as a new home for the music department to replace what is now called Pierce Hall, Sage sits at the end of the street, its elegant classicism a testimony to the importance of music in Smith's curriculum.

Correspondence between Neilson and Chester H. Aldrich began in 1922, when the college was considering a small competition between Delano and Aldrich, a firm specializing in elegant, neo-classical country houses, and Ames and Dodge, who were then working on the first buildings of the Smith Quadrangle—Jordan, Emerson, and Cushing houses. In September of 1922, the college decided that rather than compete, the two firms should work together, with Delano and Aldrich designing the music

Sage Hall

building and Ames and Dodge the new gymnasium to be built behind it. At a meeting on March 8, 1923, the two firms discussed ways to harmonize the two new buildings.

Sage, which includes a seven-hundred-seat auditorium, offices, practice rooms, and classrooms, greets the visitor with a formal, neo-classical facade at the junction of Green Street and College Lane. Four slender Ionic columns support a simple entablature that continues around the sides of the hall and a pediment that only slightly hides the dome behind. The front facade of brick is relieved by two small doors flanking the main entrance. Two-story arched windows framed by Ionic pilasters and a pediment provide plenty of natural light into the hall. The neo-classical style, reminiscent of Thomas Jefferson's work at Monticello and the University of Virginia, serves to dramatize the concert hall. Behind the hall, the class-rooms, offices, and practice rooms extend back to the south with three floors of red brick and white sash windows, whose treatment is much more practical than dramatic. At the time, the concert hall was praised for its acoustical advances. Its walls were lined with three layers of felt that were believed to enhance the quality of sound.

By the late 1980s, Sage was in need of improvements to make it technologically up to date and improve the acoustics. The renovations took place in two stages and were carried out by Polshek Partnership of New York, who later also renovated the Fine Arts Center. During the first phase of

Sage Hall, Sweeney Concert Hall

renovations the classrooms, faculty offices, and studios were updated. The building is now fully accessible and includes a new electronic music studio as well as a new green room. The second phase focused on the concert hall. The architects removed the felt walls, which actually deadened sound, and improved the acoustics. The stage was enlarged by sacrificing some seating, and video capabilities were added. Over the years the interior plasterwork had suffered a good deal of damage, and part of the renovations included repairs to the interior by local craftsman David Autio.

The decorative details carefully restored by Autio include the fluted pilasters crowned by gold-painted capitals, a lamb's tongue and pearl entablature that runs around the entire room, and an ornate frieze above the stage, which features musical motifs. Even the vents above the light

LEFT: *Tyler House*
RIGHT: *Tyler Annex*

fixtures were carefully molded in plaster. The result of this meticulous hand-work is an elegant and refined space whose architectural quality reflects the academic and cultural expertise of Smith's music department. The auditorium is named for Elsie Sweeney in gratitude for her leadership in music at Smith. Sage itself was named for Margaret Olivia Sage, who was a generous donor to Smith in the 1920s.

18. Tyler House   *William C. Brockelsby, 1898*

Addition   *David P. Handlin & Associates, 1993*

Tyler Annex   *William Fenno Pratt, 1872*

Renovations   *Alderman and MacNeish, 2002*

Tyler House is an exuberant building of red brick with curving gables and large oriel windows. Designed by Brockelsby, it epitomizes the Queen Anne style, which in America drew on colonial roots and is also known as the shingle style. The Queen Anne of Tyler House has much more in common with Newnham College (1875–1903) in Cambridge, England, however. Brockelsby likely knew of Newnham through the architectural press of the 1880s and 1890s, which was busy debating the merits of the Queen Anne style and its use in domestic and educational architecture. Newnham College, designed by Basil Champneys, exemplifies the style with a gorgeous combination of red brick buildings enlivened by white sash windows with many panes, segmented dormers and bay or oriel windows, curving gables, and decorative brickwork. Champneys wrote of this as a domestic collegiate style, appropriate for a fledgling college for women.[7]

That Brockelsby was aware of the Queen Anne style is clear from his work on Alumnae Gymnasium of 1891 with its stepped gables, decorative brickwork, and classical details used in an informal way. At Tyler House we see his interest in the Queen Anne given full rein. While the trim is now painted a pale blue, archival photographs show that the great two-story oriel windows used to be white, standing out starkly against the red brick. The curving gables that frame the building and the segmental dormers that enliven the roof are obvious quotations of Champney's design. The welcoming porch, so characteristic of Smith's cottages, is a purely American contribution, as were the shutters that originally framed the windows.[8]

Tyler House was named for William Seymour Tyler, one of the earliest trustees appointed by Sophia Smith. He graduated from and later taught at Amherst College and was an enthusiastic supporter of women's colleges, claiming that the coeducation found at places like Oberlin did not provide equal academic opportunities for women.

Tyler is a very large house, with an ell built off the back, and contained all the elements of other Smith houses, including a large dining room with a stone fireplace, a drawing room, the matron's and faculty resident's rooms, and even a sewing room.[9] In 1993, as part of the dining consolidation program, Tyler's dining room was greatly enlarged by the firm of David Handlin and Associates. Added to the west end of the building, where the original dining room had been, it now has room for residents of both Lawrence and Morris houses. The architect clearly looked to the example of Tyler Annex, a quaint cottage to the west of Tyler, for inspiration with its porch and central gable clad in the traditional New England white clapboard with forest green trim. Access to the new dining hall can be from the front or back of the addition.

Handlin's work provides a gentle segue from the towering brick of Tyler House to Tyler Annex. This small house was built in 1872 as part of a small domestic development spearheaded by the Reverend Ferry for Eliza and Augusta Seeger according to plans by William Fenno Pratt, and was purchased by Smith College in 1898. The film *Who's Afraid of Virginia Woolf* was filmed in Tyler Annex in 1965. It now houses faculty offices and was renovated in 2003.

TOP: *Smith College Club*
BOTTOM: *Smith College Club, interior*

19. Smith College Club   *William and Geoffrey Platt, 1960*

Renovations   *Leon Pernice Architects, 1984*

Renovations   *Alderman & MacNeish, 1999*

William and Geoffrey Platt designed four buildings for Smith College. In the mid-1950s they were responsible for Helen Hills Hills Chapel and Lamont House, both built in a traditional, neo-classical style. But their last buildings for Smith, Wright Hall and the Faculty Center (now known as the College Club), are strikingly modern. In fact, the College Club, which opened in 1960, was part of the college's attempt to move away from traditional forms of architecture toward contemporary styles. It signals a great change in the brothers' work.

The College Club, sitting alongside Paradise Pond, is one of the few buildings to cross College Lane. Its prime location gives it privileged access to a wooded view across the pond and to the hills beyond. The Platt brothers used modern trends in architecture to make the most of the site. The street facade is simple with an unadorned entrance and one long window breaking up the solid white brick wall. This horizontal window, which lights the kitchen area inside, has a metal screen that breaks up the wall with its filigree pattern and which is picked up again on the flat roof where it screens the utilitarian ductwork and vents. From the street, the building appears as a long, single-story rectangle attached to the older colonial revival house known simply as 51 College Lane. This is now home to offices of the Picker Engineering Program.

The juxtaposition of the traditional with the modern utilitarian is abrupt and somewhat awkward. Viewed from the pond, the two buildings are more sympathetically joined. The older colonial house has a large porch facing the pond, its roof supported by simple white columns. For the club's rear elevation the Platts opened up the rectangular box seen on College Lane into a glazed, two-story, gently bowed facade. Both floors are entirely glass, divided by slender white frames that echo the more traditional supporting columns of the older neighbor. The subtle curve of the facade further pushes the building into the privacy of the woods. An equally private terrace eases the transition between old and new.

Inside, the vast banks of windows light an easily divided dining room on the first floor and lounges on the lower, basement floor. Recent renovations increased accessibility with an entrance ramp and elevator, and enlarged the kitchen facilities. Visitors enter the building via a low-ceilinged foyer that leads into the much more dramatic dining space, whose great glass walls bring diners virtually into the surrounding woods. With its planned flexibility of rooms and gorgeous views of the changing seasons, the College Club provides a warm and versatile environment for academic discourse and interaction.

20. Burton Hall *Charles A. Rich, 1914*

The advancement of women in the sciences has been a concern of Smith College for decades. Lilly Hall, one of Smith's earliest buildings, was the college's first home for the sciences, exposing women to scientific subjects and methods. As early as 1905 a committee, which included Seelye and several faculty members, called for a new science building to relieve the overcrowding of Lilly Hall, agreeing that Lilly should contain physics and geology, but the life sciences such as zoology, botany, and physiology needed a new home. Of great interest were the reasons they gave:

> The need for a new biological building, however, does not arise solely, or even primarily, from the obvious necessity of better facilities for present work, but from a more important consideration. The college recognizes it as a duty and privilege not simply to follow traditional lines of teaching, but to endeavor to discover through investigation and experiment the education which is of most worth for women. It is its belief that Biology—in its broadest and most liberal sense—dealing as that science does with the origin, development and processes of life, is a peculiarly valuable and appropriate study in a college for women.[10]

While such a reason—that women should study biology because of their reproductive abilities—seems outlandish today, educators in the years before World War I were very concerned with the "nature of women" and how to reconcile it with their academic abilities. Twenty-five years earlier, they faced the challenge of proving that women could achieve the same academic results as men and remain healthy and feminine. By 1905 women's colleges found themselves integrating domestic science and reproduction into their curricula to silence new critics who feared for the state of the family.

Thus Burton Hall was built in what became a new quad. Facing the rear of Neilson Library, it was designed by Charles A. Rich, the architect of Barnard's main building, John Greene Hall, and Northrop and Gillett houses at Smith. Clad in Smith's traditional red brick, it was built of steel and concrete for fire reasons. Classical details of brownstone and terra cotta elaborate the long, horizontal building. The front facade, articulated by regular ranges of windows on all three floors, has a vigorous entrance with stocky Ionic pilasters supporting a heavy curving pediment. Above, extending the height of the second and third floors are four Ionic pilasters separated by shallow balustrades on the second floor and decorative terra cotta swags on the third. A heavy entablature and stringcourse wrap around the entire building. It is a solid and imposing neo-classical building softened only by the arch above the door and the graceful swags that we see on other Smith buildings such as Alumnae Gym.

Burton Hall

When it was first opened, Burton Hall had a large lecture room, seating about three hundred, offices, smaller lecture rooms, laboratories, museum or exhibit space, and storerooms. In 1929 a small addition was added behind the hall to house live animals needed for study. Many more changes were ahead for the building with the development of the Clark Science Center. Today, Burton's relatively quiet entrance lobby greets the visitor with *Aperiodic Penrose a* by sculptor and mathematician Helman Ferguson. A beautiful and tactile scupture, it illustrates a mathematical theorem, challenging the mind as well as the eye.

21. Clark Science Center

Sabin-Reed Hall *Shepley, Bulfinch, Richardson and Abbott, 1967*

McConnell Hall *Shepley, Bulfinch, Richardson and Abbott, 1967*

Renovations *Shepley, Bulfinch, Richardson and Abbott, 1991*

Under the presidency of Mendenhall, the role of the sciences at Smith was once more under discussion. No longer were the faculty and administration concerned with what sciences were appropriate for women. Instead, the focus was on encouraging women to major in the sciences, attract top faculty, and to encourage non-majors to enroll in science classes to broaden their understanding of the world around them. Characteristic of Mendenhall's approach to new building campaigns, the discussion he began included important input from faculty. By early 1961 the first draft of the "President's Science Fund" outlined their goals and stressed the interrelatedness of the scienctific fields. Basic to the scheme were the renovation of Burton Hall; the need for a new building to house the physical sciences such as physics, chemistry, geology, astronomy, and math; and a building that connected the two and included a science library. Once these aims were decided upon, Mendenhall began his search for architects. He was most impressed with the work of the firm of Shepley, Bulfinch, Richardson and Abbott, who had recently completed work at the Woods Hole Marine Biological Laboratory and came highly recommended by its director there.

In July of 1961, still early in the design process, Richardson wrote to Mendenhall that while faculty members were being interviewed,

> we are making mass studies both in drawings and models. As you know, we are greatly concerned about the bulk of building required in such a central location on the campus. We are hopeful of arriving at a scheme which not only meets the program but maintains the domestic character of Smith College.[11]

The site chosen was behind and beside Burton Hall, which required the demolition of the old Students' Building. Due to its inclusive nature, the center, named for Avon Cosmetics heiress Edna McConnell Clark (class of 1909) and her husband W. Van Allan Clark, was at the time the biggest building project a women's college had ever undertaken.[12] The Clarks donated $3 million of the $8 million needed for the project, and McConnell Hall, which housed the departments of astronomy, physics, and mathematics, was named after Edna Clark's father. The second building, Sabin-Reed Hall, accommodating the departments of bacteriology, botany, chemistry, zoology, and the Science Library, was named for two distinguished Smith alumnae: Florence Sabin, class of 1893, had been the first woman to become professor at Johns Hopkins and received a fellowship at

Sabin–Reed and McConnell Halls

the Rockefeller Institute of Medical Research. Mendenhall's mother, Dr. Dorothy Reed Mendenhall, class of 1895, was a fellow at Johns Hopkins who conducted important medical research in childhood diseases and discovered the diagnosis for Hodgkins Disease.

The very large, four-story building is sited just behind Burton Hall and extends beyond it to the north and south. It connects to Burton via a dramatic concrete staircase with an elevator shaft clad in blue and turquoise glass tiles at its center. While Sabin-Reed is relatively unobtrusive from the Science Quad, its monumentality is evident along College Lane. Here solid brick walls are divided into ten bays by long vertical windows and concrete shafts with brick in-fill. Cast-concrete panels between each brick shaft articulate a rhythm down the facade. A large concrete cornice crowns the building.

McConnell Hall sits perpendicular to Burton and Sabin-Reed and is connected via a two-story glass bridge. Though smaller in scale, its brick walls are also divided into bays by tall vertical windows that extend to the second, third, and fourth floors. The first floor is articulated by stocky concrete columns and tinted glass; just inside the entrance is a foyer that provides space for student projects and round tables, its empty walls often holding students' posters of their scientific work. While the site and the materials used for these two structures downplay the otherwise monumental building scheme, the whole complex testifies to the importance of the study of science at Smith.

Bass Hall

22. Bass Hall and Young Science Library

Shepley, Bulfinch, Richardson and Abbott, 1991

The addition of Bass Hall and the Young Science Library, both opened in 1991, marks the continued growth of the sciences at Smith. Less than thirty years after the completion of the Clark Science Center, faculty and students were complaining about overcrowding and inadequate facilities. President Mary Maples Dunn recognized the problem and began to address it in the late 1980s. As early as 1983, a Science Planning Committee was formed to look into the growth of the sciences at Smith and in 1985 the firm of Shepley, Bulfinch, Richardson and Abbott was called in to discuss plans for a new building.

A site to the east of McConnell Hall was chosen to form a quadrangle with Neilson, Burton, and Wright halls. Though the loss of a part of Burton Lawn was a concern of many, Helen Searing, a professor of architectural history at Smith, reassured Dunn: "Rather than violating Burton Lawn's integrity, I see the scheme as making a positive impact by defining the lawn on the fourth side so that it no longer visually leaks toward Green Street."[13]

The new building was to house not only the entire psychology department and a new computer center, but also the vast and ever-growing science library. Since its scale had to match that of the surrounding buildings—not only the Clark Science Center and Neilson Library but also Morris and Lawrence houses—it was divided into two distinct but connected units. The larger one, funded by Anne T. and Robert M. Bass, after whom it is named, houses the psychology department and computer center, while the smaller unit comprises the library, named in honor of the Robert R. Young Foundation, which contributed to its funding.

Young Science Library

The primary architect at Shepley, Bulfinch, Richardson and Abbott involved in the project was Jean Paul Carlhian, who with Bass Hall and the Young Library succeeded in producing new high-tech structures that harmonize effectively with their neighbors. His designs show clear evidence of postmodernism. Both buildings are clad in Smith's characteristic red brick with Indiana limestone details. Traditional elements such as stringcourses, window lintels, ocular windows, and dormers are found throughout both buildings. Yet some traditional elements are handled with a modern flair such as the stringcourse that encircles the building where it meets the ground. Not only is this an unexpected place for a stringcourse, but its bulbous shape toys further with our expectations. The main entrance to Bass Hall is dramatized by powerful squat doric columns and narrow slit windows above the door.

The Young Science Library is generally accessed through Bass Hall. It is built in a cruciform shape with gently sloping gables that echo those of Morris and Lawrence houses next door. Its graceful cupola and spindly weather vane tie it to Alumnae Gym and flood the second and third floors with light. Overall, the scheme sits comfortably in a tight location.

Less comfortable are the temporary headquarters of the fledgling engineering program. This green rectangular building, which hides behind Bass Hall and connects with the Science Library, was designed by R. E. Dinneen Architects & Planners of Boston and completed in 2000.

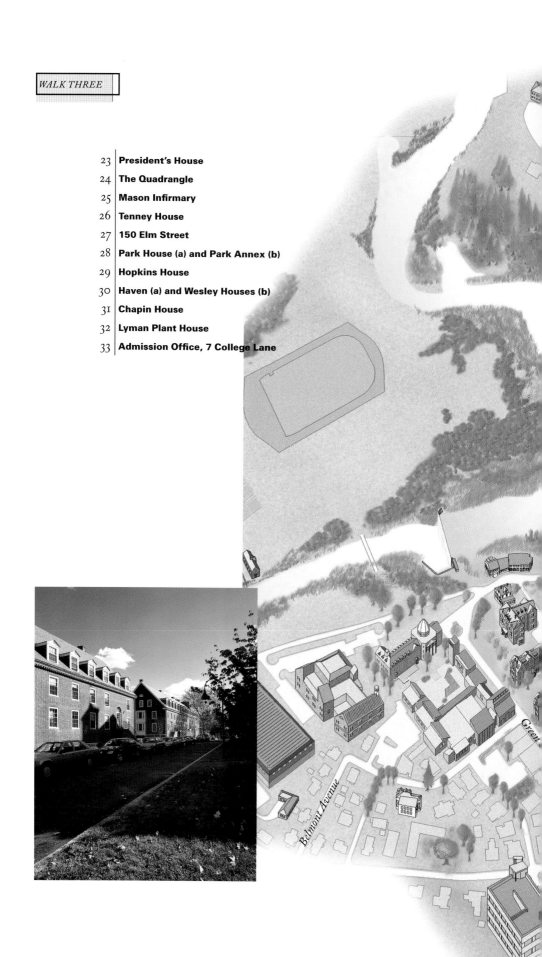

Belmont Avenue

Green

23. President's House *John W. Ames, 1920*

In 1917, as part of an enticement package to lure William Allen Neilson to Smith as president, the college promised to build a new president's house. It took some time to raise the money for a house of the size and grandeur necessary, but by 1920 Neilson and his family had moved into their new accommodations. In contrast to the very public siting of Gateway, the original house for the president, this house sits on the western edge of campus behind a row of houses that front Elm Street and alongside the picturesque gardens and paths that fringe Paradise Pond and the Mill River. It has a formal public front and a relatively private rear facade. Visitors and students walking to classes from the Quad are greeted by a rectangular neo-Georgian block with green colonial shutters framing the tall windows of the first and second floors. For this important house the architect, John W. Ames, broke with tradition and abandoned the usual red brick in favor of a creamy, off-white stucco. This serves to differentiate the President's House from the students' residences, while the neo-Georgian style keeps it visually tied to the nearby Quadrangle.

Ames was a personal friend of Neilson, whom he knew from Cambridge, Massachusetts; he later worked with his partner Edwin Sherrill Dodge and Smith's own Karl Putnam (architect of the 1938 wing of the library) on the enormous quadrangle project. For Neilson, Ames designed a house that elegantly meets the public and private needs of the president. The central block is framed by two-story white Ionic pilasters, which highlight the entrance and frame the doorway and arched window on the second floor. The regularity of the front is softened in the rear by gently curving bow windows and a central stoa supported by Ionic columns. French doors lead the visitor out from the foyer to the garden, where a shady allée leads toward the river. The house was illustrated in *House Beautiful* in 1921, where it was praised for the subtle blending of public and private spaces.[1]

On the first floor, a large foyer provides access to the gracious living room to the right and an equally elegant dining room to the left. All three accommodate formal entertaining, from small musical recitals performed in the foyer, to large dinner parties in the grand dining room. Both the dining and living rooms have bow windows on the west side that reach out and embrace the spectacular views of Paradise Pond and the Holyoke Range. The kitchen, accessed through the dining room, was renovated in the 1990s. The formal interior spaces have been redecorated many times over the years, often with help from the trustees. The artwork that hangs on walls throughout the house is all by Smith faculty.

OPPOSITE: *President's House*

President's House

In addition to these grand spaces, the house also includes smaller rooms in which the president and her/his family can feel more at home. A sunroom to the south of the dining room offers spectacular views of the garden and mountains beyond and provides a perfect space for more intimate dining. The second-floor bedrooms and studies are reserved for the family with the exception of visitors from the Board of Trustees. These rooms can be reached by a private back staircase or via the more public grand central stair. The President's House offers both a welcome haven amid the bustle of college life and a gracious venue in which to entertain official visitors.

24. The Quadrangle

Emerson House, Cushing House, Jordan House *Ames, Dodge and Putnam, 1922*

Morrow House, Gardiner House, Wilson House *Ames, Dodge and Putnam, 1926*

Renovation *Alderman & MacNeish, 1996*

Wilder House and Comstock House *Ames, Dodge and Putnam, 1930*

Renovation *Juster Pope Frazier, 2000*

Laura Scales House and Franklin King House *Ames, Dodge and Putnam, 1936*

Renovation *Dietz & Company, 2001*

For years, Smith set a precedent for small-scale housing on women's college campuses, favoring the cottage system over the great institutional buildings of Vassar and Wellesley well into the first decade of the twentieth century. Yet by the time Neilson took over as president in 1917, the domestic, small-scale nature of Smith's cottages proved unable to fill the college's housing needs. Most students lived off campus in boarding houses. Both Dean Comstock and President Neilson were concerned that this situation was hurting the Smith community. Not only did it deprive off-campus residents of the intellectual exchanges that living under one roof stimulated, but it was also deemed undemocratic. Women with few financial advantages lived poorly, while those with ample funds dwelt in comfort.[2] On-campus housing, on the other hand, would offer opportunities for students of different financial means and backgrounds to meet and get to know one another. The college's wish to house all of Smith's students led to the building of the quadrangle.

Pleased with Ames's work for the new president's house, Neilson hired the architect to work up schemes for these new residences. This time he teamed up with Edwin Sherrill Dodge, another Boston architect, who had worked on educational buildings before. For the first three houses, a local architect, Karl Putnam, also collaborated. Putnam later went on to teach at

Wilson House

Smith and to design the first wing of the library in 1938. The greatest challenge these architects faced was how to house a great number of women while avoiding the dull monotony of large institutional buildings. In the tradition of the old Oxbridge colleges in England, large quadrangles were planned but in a neo-Georgian style. This style was more affordable than a collegiate Gothic and was evocative of old New England colonial buildings and the academia of Harvard Yard.

The first house to be built was Ellen Emerson, which fronts Paradise Road almost directly opposite the driveway of President's House. An arched gateway through the house gave access to the large quadrangle, which would, by 1926, include Jordan, Cushing, Morrow, Gardiner, and Wilson houses. This central arch is flanked by two small pedestrian entries, all three of which are highlighted by central keystones. The red brick, laid in a Flemish bond pattern, is enlivened by a white stone stringcourse and paired Ionic pilasters framing the central windows. From this rectangular block extend smaller, three-story wings, treated with stucco rather than brick, which house the kitchens and service areas of the building. Stretching north from these arms run Cushing to the east and Jordan to the west. They both continue the simple but elegant neo-Georgian style with graceful, shallow two-story oriel windows trimmed in white on their northern ends.

The plans of the buildings are also similar. The ground floor of Emerson has a reception room just inside the door leading into the dining room to the left of the entrance arch. This is serviced by a kitchen where

Laura Scales House

food was prepared for both Emerson and Cushing (which had a separate dining room). There were several residential rooms for servants, who were expected to live in the dormitories in which they worked. To the right of the arch is another reception foyer with stairs to the upper floors, a living room with a fireplace, and access to the house matron's parlor. Further along in the stuccoed wings were two parlors, a visitor's suite, and separate dining room, as well as the kitchen that served Jordan House. It was intended that most of a woman's social life would happen in these ground-floor public rooms. Indeed, when Scales and King houses were built, some of these public spaces were referred to as "beau parlors," where students could entertain their male guests.[3] On the upper floors long corridors provide access to the students' rooms. The size of these rooms varied little, adding to the democratic nature of this new residential system.

Elegant cut-back stairs of brick and stone break open the quadrangle and lead to King and Scales to the east and Wilder and Comstock houses to the west. Morrow and Gardiner houses continue the long arms of the quadrangle and mirror Cushing and Jordan architecturally. Wilson, at the north end of the quadrangle, is the most elaborate of these houses, with a great central tower protruding from the rest of the building and a large white cupola with details borrowed from Sir Christopher Wren's designs.[4] The dramatic, large rectangular central block is flanked by two-story curving arms that hold the kitchens and end in gabled, one-story dining rooms. The ensemble is a delightful blend of gentle arches, ocular windows, and Ionic pilasters, which add lively variety to the otherwise simple dormitory blocks.

To the west of the main quadrangle lie Comstock and Wilder houses, opened in 1930. These two dorms form an independent quadrangle and are the simplest of the quadrangle buildings, with a pared-down neo-Georgian design in the two main blocks and more elaborate details reserved for the central entrance arch. Here a shallow oriel window rises three stories above the Palladian archway. It is interesting to note that this tight little quad

TOP: *Franklin King House*
BOTTOM: *Wilder House*

Wilder House

departs from its English prototype in one particular way. Whereas most English collegiate quads have entryways from within the quadrangle, those of Comstock and Wilder face the rest of the campus. This decreases the cloister-like effect that many quadrangles have and affirms the houses' connection to campus.

The final phase of this massive effort to house all of Smith's students came with the building of King and Scales houses in 1936. These two buildings sit opposite Wilder and Comstock and provide balance to the whole. But where Wilder and Comstock have a quiet simplicity, King and Scales with their dramatic curve and lively Georgian details are exuberant as their great arms hug the landscape and reach out toward their neighbors. Looking up into the semi-circle one is reminded of the curving terraces of Bath, England, with their elegant Georgian domesticity. Bow windows on the first floor begin the stretch inward toward the central block. Along the way, fluted white pilasters frame the full-length windows of the public rooms. In the center block, the curves of the fanlights above the dining-room windows are echoed in the two curving gables of the roofline. White Ionic

Mason Infirmary

pilasters mark out a rhythm between the central windows. As with Comstock and Wilder, most students enter and leave through doors on the outside of the curve, but the inner quad with its lush shade trees and outdoor patio for eating make it an enticing public space.

    The quadrangles were a dramatic shift for the college, introducing formal axes and drawing on a distinct collegiate precedent. The resulting ensemble is a comfortable blend of public and private spaces all housed in a gracious cloak of red brick and white trim classicism that is both warm and welcoming, while formal and dramatic.

25. Mason Infirmary *Taylor and Putnam, 1919*

Additions *Coolidge, Shepley, Bulfinch and Abbott, 1942 and 1951*

Before the widespread use of successful vaccines, a college infirmary was needed to isolate infected students and prevent the spread of disease. Accordingly, such a space has been a part of Smith since 1888, when the college physician, Dr. Preston, used a vacant house near campus to treat students. By 1898 two houses on College Lane were purchased, one as an infirmary and the other to house students in case of an epidemic. Sunnyside, at the end of Paradise Road, was given by Mrs. John S. Cobb in 1905 and was used to house ill students, but this was not ideal as its residents had to leave their house to accommodate their sick classmates. During President Burton's tenure, more attention was paid to the idea of having a proper infirmary, but it was not until after the 1918 flu epidemic that a purpose-built infirmary was finally constructed.

OPPOSITE: *Gardiner and Jordan houses, with King and Scales houses in the background*

The local firm of Taylor and Putnam designed a building cloaked in a restrained neo-Georgian classicism and tucked away on the edge of campus along Paradise Road. The infirmary was named for Elizabeth Mason Howland (class of 1904), whose parents provided part of the funds for the building. The architects continued the use of red brick with white stone dressing seen in so many college buildings. Classical keystones dramatize the windows, while the rectangular severity of these brick blocks is softened by the curving pediment over the main entrance, the full-length semi-circular window above the east-wing's entrance, and the cheerful curved dormers on the roof.

The original building was laid out on an irregular H-plan with a wing to the rear of the building extending out three bays to the east. It could accommodate thirty-six beds and had a full-time resident physician. As part of its participation in the war effort, Smith became the home for the WAVES (Women Appointed for Voluntary Emergency Service) training program in 1941. This required more infirmary space for which the Navy helped pay. A fund-raising campaign provided the college with enough money to build the first two floors of a three-story wing to the west of the main building. The well-known firm of Coolidge, Shepley, Bulfinch and Abbott, who were responsible for many buildings at Harvard, designed the addition, which included X-Ray equipment, a small surgery space, and a laboratory, in a very simplified neo-Georgian style. The Navy also built a temporary wooden structure, which was dismantled after the war.

By the 1950s, with a head physician and four other full-time physicians on staff, the infirmary could accommodate sixty students and ninety in a crisis. The Infirmary Committee, led by Mary Ellen Chase, invited visitors to see their cheerful facilities:

> When you are next in Northampton, come to visit this red brick building among its woods and above its river. Once you have seen its quiet tasteful rooms, its books, its kitchens, its gathering places for games, talks, and study, and have felt the home-like atmosphere within its walls, you will understand why many of us look upon it as one of the greatest blessings of our college community.[5]

Although contagious diseases are today not as much a concern as they were in the past, the infirmary is still an active and busy place offering a wide range of medical services, counseling, and health education.

26. Tenney House *Architect unknown, 1881*

Renovation *Alderman & MacNeish, 2000*

From its earliest days, Smith College has aimed to offer higher education to women without substantial financial means. One of the first organized efforts to accommodate these students was undertaken by Mary Smith Tenney. Tenney was originally from Northampton but had moved to Ohio with her husband where she ran a girls' school. After she returned to Northampton, she opened her family house, 33 Elm Street, to Smith College students in 1895. She was particularly concerned about students of lesser means who often had to live in undesirable housing off-campus in order to attend college. For these students she began to provide rooms at a reduced rate, asking them to participate in the housekeeping duties of the house and help prepare meals in exchange. This cooperative experiment became official in 1895 when Tenney and her brother Justin Smith left their house and the land behind it to the college. In her will Tenney required that some rooms in her home be reserved for students who could not afford the full cost of college board and that they participate in household duties. The small cooperative was extremely successful and was held up as a model in 1910 when Lawrence House also became a co-op.

Tenney House was located at the head of Elm Street until 1937, when termites got the better of its eighteenth-century walls and it was torn down to make way for Alumnae House. The Tenney co-op experiment then moved to 156 Elm Street, at the corner of Paradise Road and Elm Street, into a house built in 1881 for James Ward. Number 156 Elm had served as the parsonage of St. John's Church, before the college bought it in 1916. A typical shingle-style building, Tenney House has colonial details with shutters and clapboard siding, strong gables, an open entrance porch, and a large bank of small-paned windows on the first floor. In the summer of 2000 it was renovated by Alderman & MacNeish of West Springfield. Thermal-pane windows replaced the old drafty ones, and the first floor was made fully accessible. Along with mechanical updates, the bathrooms were renovated and a new kitchen installed.

150 Elm Street with Tenney House beyond

27. 150 Elm Street   *Architect unknown, 1884*

Renovation   *Alderman & MacNeish, 1997*

Number 150 Elm Street graces this important thoroughfare with Victorian charm. The symmetrical block, which features an entrance porch with a decorative balcony on top, is embellished by large shuttered windows on the first and second floors and crowned by steeply pitched dormer windows with delicate curvilinear design insets on the third. The deep eaves of the roof are supported by decorative brackets. Before the college purchased the house in 1917, it was owned by Clara Allen, who kept a small gift shop and tea room there. Originally, the college used the house for overflow students during the first semester, housing them more permanently in the second semester.

In 1997, 150 Elm was renovated by the local firm of Alderman & MacNeish, who upgraded the bathrooms and a kitchenette and installed a sophisticated heating system as part of Smith's Energy Management System. This has saved energy and given the students the ability to adjust the heat in their rooms according to their own comfort levels.

Houses such as 150 Elm contribute to the campus's unique residential feel. While belonging to the campus, the house appears to be part of the neighborhood, architecturally blurring the distinction between town and gown. This visual melding is part of what the founders wished for as they sent their students into Northampton for church services and to the library, assuring that the campus not become an isolating force in the women's lives.

Park House *William Fenno Pratt, 1880*

Addition *Architect unknown, 1920*

Park Annex, formerly Look House *Architect unknown, 1892*

In the 1920s, the campus grew rapidly with the building of the dormitory quadrangles. As part of President Neilson's efforts to house all students on campus, nearby houses continued to be purchased as student residences. Park House and Park Annex were two such houses bought by the college in 1920 and together accommodated fifty-nine students.

Park House was built in 1880 by the locally famous William Fenno Pratt, a versatile architect who was comfortable designing houses in a variety of styles, often modeled on the nineteenth-century architect's bibles of vernacular architecture, *Cottage Residences* (1842) and *The Architecture of Country Houses* (1850), both by Andrew Jackson Downing. Downing illustrated a wide range of domestic styles and floor plans that influenced architects throughout the nineteenth century. For the manufacturer W. T. Clement, Pratt built in a simplified Gothic style with elaborate brick detailing in the stringcourses and chimneys but without the picturesque and varied floor plan and silhouette so characteristic of Victorian Gothic. A heavy corbelled entablature and arched brick dormers divide the second and third stories, while white trim and pale stone enliven the windows and porches. Entry is through a south-facing porch with a now enclosed porch above. Park House stands out from its nearby residential neighbors with their clapboard and shingle siding, but its lively red brick ties it to the majority of Smith's buildings.

It was perhaps in an attempt to blend Park House with its wooden neighbors that the addition of 1920 was clad in clapboard. This very regular, functional wing increased the population of Park House considerably, yet did little to harmonize with the enthusiastic brick original. But in 1925, Katharine S. Stebbins, in her history of Park House reported that:

> Park House was an especially good place to live during the spring months with its lovely view of Paradise Pond, the hill opposite and Mt. Tom in the distance, and even during a very hot week the first of June, the upper porches gave us what little air there was and we could almost forget final exams and the heat.[6]

Park Annex was built in 1892 for Dwight Look, a member of the respectable Northampton Look family after whom Look Park is named. For many years after Look died, Miss Frances Look, his daughter, lived there. She and her neighbor, Miss Elizabeth Maltby, opened their houses as off-campus residences for Smith students, and until it was sold to Smith in

TOP: *Park House*
BOTTOM: *Park Annex*

1920, Look House, also known as "Perch," was part of the famous Miss Maltby's houses. These houses were always popular off-campus residences and were easily converted to campus residences after they were purchased by the college.

The unknown architect of Park Annex designed the house in the shingle style. The facade facing Elm Street has a large pedimented entrance porch that wraps around to the north side. To the left of the door is a five-sided, two-story bay window that dramatically opens the rectangular box. A large shingled gable, lit by a Palladian window in the center, stretches across the front of the house. On the south side is another entrance with an open porch and a shallow bay window in the third-story gable. A jubilant motif that looks like a rising sun, its rays stretching out to fill the rectangle, decorates the gable. The house is a delightful blend of masses and voids, with contrasting textures in the clapboards of the first floor and the scalloped shingles above. Its irregular outline and original leaded glass windows suggest cozy intimate spaces within.

29. Hopkins House *William Fenno Pratt, 1861*

Renovation *Kuhn Riddle Architects, 2000*

Like its neighbor, Park Annex, Hopkins House was originally built for a respectable Northampton family. When Miss Elizabeth Maltby bought it from the original owner, Jonathan Huntington Lyman, in 1898, it became yet another off-campus house for Smith students. Miss Maltby was famous for her expansive personality and lively entertaining, and her house was extremely popular with Smith students. So popular, in fact, that by 1910 she had built two more houses just behind Hopkins, which were known for years as Hopkins A and Hopkins B. (While Miss Maltby ran her lodgings, the original house was called "Feathers," Hopkins A was known as "Quill," and Hopkins B as "Owl's Nest.")

After running these successful residences for eighteen years, Maltby offered to sell them to Smith, and four years later President Neilson accepted the offer as part of his effort to house all students on campus. The college acquired all three houses and named them after Elizabeth Jarvis Hopkins, who had been the house matron of Dewey House for the first fifteen years of the college and whose wisdom and social skills were important factors in the early success of the college. As one alumna put it:

> Mrs. Hopkins' official connection with the College covered those formative years when its reputation was still in the making and when college ideals for women were still tentative....To scholarship, to womanhood, she labored to add...the old-fashioned and rare qualities of the true lady.[7]

Hopkins House

Not only was Hopkins's influence important socially, but the building that carries her name is one of Northampton and Smith's architectural gems. Built by Pratt in 1861, it is a striking blend of architectural styles. The central symmetrical block is crowned by a mansard roof, both elements associated with a French Second Empire style. Yet the surface is enlivened by pointed arches that interrupt the roofline and frame arched windows with tracery, typical of the Gothic revival. The shutters, pointed on the second floor, add a touch of the colonial to the mix. Bow windows and tiny dormers provide variety. The building is enveloped in smooth wooden cladding.

Over the years Hopkins House has stretched out toward campus and away from Elm Street. Most recently, in the Summer of 2001, Kuhn Riddle Architects of Amherst, Massachusetts, carried out extensive renovations, adding a porch and an accessible entrance on the north side and re-using some of the old millwork salvaged from the demolition of Hopkins A and B, which were torn down in 1999. These two buildings had become structurally unsound as their foundations had shifted. Where they once stood there is now a green lawn overlooking the Lyman Plant houses and Paradise Pond.

Haven House

30. Haven and Wesley Houses

Haven   *architect unknown, 1865*

Addition   *Rand and Skinner, 1902*

Wesley House   *Curtis G. Page, 1896*

Addition, renovation, and relocation   *Kuhn Riddle Architects, 2000*

Haven and Wesley houses have always shared a close relationship, which evolved out of their proximity to one another. Student government, parties, and house projects have been joint ventures, but the two houses present very different faces to the campus. Haven was built in 1865 and is one of the many residences along Elm Street that Smith acquired to house its students. When the college bought it in 1899, it was a modest, three-story, almost square house. The clapboard siding gives way on the third floor to a solid wooden envelope with rectangular moldings between the windows. Across the Elm Street facade a porch shelters visitors, its shallow roof supported by gently curving brackets.

In 1902, with some of the new funds from a Rockefeller grant and alumnae donations, Haven was greatly enlarged by the firm of Rand and Skinner from Boston, who also built Smith's Chapin House and Mead Hall at Mount Holyoke College. This sensitive scheme tripled the size of the house, extending back from Elm Street into the campus. A two-story veranda welcomes the visitor, its graceful Doric columns interrupted by a balcony on the second floor. A large rectangular block, which mirrors in detail the original house, completes the addition. While not perfectly symmetrical, the extension to Haven is balanced and gracious. It also realigned the house,

Chapin House

diminishing the importance of the Elm Street entrance and focusing on the life of the inner campus. Haven's great porches now look directly onto the new Campus Center, one of the college's major arteries.

Wesley House originally nestled behind Haven where the new Campus Center is now. Built in 1896 by the local architect Curtis G. Page (architect of the First National Bank Building in Northampton) as the rectory for the Methodist Church on Elm Street, the college acquired it in 1899. Next to Haven's long rectangular blocks and uninterrupted rooflines, Wesley appears busy with its picturesque arrangement of gables, dormers, and porches, which add variety and indicate cozy, intimate spaces within. The house was moved in 2000 in order to make room for the Campus Center and now sits just to the northwest of Haven, still close to its big sister.

31. Chapin House *Rand and Skinner, 1903*

Renovation *Juster Pope Frazier, 1996*

In 1902 the growth and success of Smith College was rewarded by a Rockefeller grant for the generous sum of $100,000. This gift, together with another $100,000 raised by alumnae and friends of the college, sparked a new building campaign that included the Students' Building (now demolished) and Chapin House, another large residence for Smith's burgeoning population. It was named after Henrietta Chapin Seelye, the president's wife, to honor her steady and devoted commitment to the college.

Lyman Plant House

Residents of Chapin find themselves living in the heart of the campus, a short distance to the Science Quad just behind them and Seelye Quad to their right. The new Campus Center is also a stone's throw away. Chapin commands spectacular views of Paradise Pond and the mountains beyond. Perhaps in keeping with its ideal location, Chapin introduced a formal classical architecture to Smith's halls of residence that would continue to be popular for the next forty years. It is a stately block of red brick with white trim and keystones over the windows. The corners are strongly defined by brick quoins, and the entrance is emphasized by a grand two-story porch with slender, paired, Ionic columns. Ocular windows light the two gables, and cheerful pedimented dormers punctuate the roof. On the back facade a semi-circular panel with a Palladian window breaks the regular rhythm of the windows and indicates the stairway within.

Inside, the first floor had a remarkably open floor plan for the time, with the entrance hall flowing freely into the dining room to the right and a reception room to the left. The latter room was visually broken into two by half-height walls with columns that reached to the ceiling, giving a sense of intimacy to the smaller portion without breaking up the spacious quality of the room. Along the backside of the house were the kitchens and service spaces as well as rooms for the faculty resident and the matron.

Lyman Plant House, interior

32. Lyman Plant House

Greenhouses *Lord & Burnham Manufacturers, 1895*

Wooden houses replaced by brick *Architect unknown, 1904*

Renovations *Alderman & MacNeish, 1981*

Addition *Perry Dean Rogers & Partners, 2002–03*

As Smith's population grew in the 1890s, the landscape and arrangement of buildings on campus became a major concern of President Seelye. The firm of Olmsted & Eliot drew up plans for the growth of the college in 1893. As part of this work, the plantings on campus became increasingly important. Seelye envisioned the campus as a great arboretum, an outdoor botany classroom that included plants and trees from around the world and afforded students both pleasure and an education as they strolled the college grounds.[8] Two small wooden houses along College Lane were acquired and housed the fledgling botany department. In 1894 the college hired William Ganong, a highly respected professor of botany who had been at Harvard's Botanic Gardens. Thanks to his energy and direction, the college soon had a large complex of greenhouses, including the Palm House, a fern house, and a succulent house, all built by the firm of Lord & Burnham, well-known manufacturers of greenhouses. The prominent Northampton Lyman family gave money for the greenhouses in honor of Anne Jean Lyman. E. H. R. Lyman, her son, gave the initial sum and later in 1902 and 1904 his children donated more funds for the building's expansion.

The original greenhouses are descendants of a noble tradition of greenhouse design, most notably from the greenhouses of Kew Gardens outside London, designed by Decimus Burton and Richard Turner between 1845 and 1847. A long simple range extends out from the brick houses and culminates in the Palm House with its dramatic curving roof, its thin glass membrane articulated by a skeletal metal frame. An elegant fanlight above the door highlights a glass entrance porch, which is no longer used. The entire complex is crowned by an iron filigree roof ridge, painted white, which looks lacy against a bright blue sky. The plant house also includes the Succulent House, Palm House, Cool Temperate House, Warm Temperate House, and Stove House. The brick houses that front College Lane are in the tradition of early buildings at Smith, with a tile-hung gable above the main door and a charming timbered porch elaborating the facades.

The Lyman Plant House has continued to grow throughout the twentieth century and on into the twenty-first. In the 1950s, under the direction of Dr. Albert F. Blakeslee, it was an important Genetics Experiment Station with two new ranges built along the northwest side of the plant house. In 1981 the firm of Alderman & MacNeish replaced these with a large greenhouse and laboratories.

In 2002 and 2003 Perry Dean Rogers and Partners of Boston carried out renovation work and designed a major addition, which included new office space for the administration as well as a new classroom, room for bulb storage, research areas, public bathrooms, and a manager's office. The main administrative wing extends north from the brick houses and is a simple block of uncomplicated post and lintel framing with large windows lighting the interior. A glass corridor connects this wing with a subterranean addition, which was built into the hillside and takes the visitor by surprise as it modestly hides beneath a rooftop lawn. This latest addition is a subtle blend of earth, glass, steel, and sky and unites the old with the new in a seamless continuum. The plant houses and the study of botany continue to be an important part of Smith College and students still benefit from Seelye's vision of an arboretum within the campus boundaries.

Admission Office

33. Admission Office, 7 College Lane

William Fenno Pratt, c. 1861

Renovation *David P. Handlin & Associates, 1993*

Originally located on Elm Street, 7 College Lane was built in 1861 by Pratt for the widow of E. G. Stoddard. Smith purchased the house in 1888 and rented it until 1909 when the land it was on was needed for the building of John M. Greene Hall. The house was then moved to its present location on College Lane. For almost a century this modest residence had a variety of occupants, from the head gardener, Franklin King, to a series of deans, directors of buildings and grounds, and briefly serving as the home for the Department of Religion from 1950 to 1952.

In 1993 the college hired David Handlin to renovate the house as the new Office of Admission. His goal was to maintain the domestic nature of the building while organizing the interior to comfortably house offices and welcome prospective students. Admission had previously been on West Street in Garrison Hall, but the central location at the top of College Lane had obvious advantages. To make the house accommodate its new purpose, Handlin enlarged its footprint and dug out the basement for added space. A small wing for an elevator and service spaces was added to the north of the

house. Before the renovations, the house had been "oblivious to the view."[9]
A spacious waiting room now looks out over Paradise Pond and the hills
beyond. To emphasize this vista, a porch was also added.

The modest house has white clapboard siding. Two gabled ends,
each with its own entrance, face College Lane and the visitors' parking lot,
respectively. In the gables, arched windows covered with green shutters and
decorated with a pointed arched molding add charming details. Simple
Doric columns support the entrance porches. To the west, the one-story
extension that houses the waiting room is set off from the older portion by
its beige clapboards and white trim.

The use of No. 7 College Lane for the Office of Admission is particularly fitting, as the house introduces visitors to the warm domesticity that is
so much a part of life at Smith and emphasizes the spectacular natural
beauty that surrounds the college.

Paradise Road

Elm Street

Round Hill Road

37

34

35

36

44

45

Henshaw Avenue

College Lane

40b

40a

39

43

42

38

41

Prospect Street

Bedford Terrace

34. Helen Hills Hills Chapel *William and Geoffrey Platt, 1955*

Addition *Kuhn Riddle Architects, 2002*

The absence of a purpose-built chapel at the early college was partly due to the ideals of the founders, who wanted Smith students to be a part of the Northampton community and attend the local churches. But the addition of a chapel was often discussed, and in 1933 Ames and Dodge presented a drawing of a chapel of red brick with white trim, very much in the style of their work on the Quadrangle. In 1935 the college hired its first chaplain and the need for a chapel, albeit a small one, was pressing. Surprisingly, this need was met in the first wing of the Neilson Library of 1938, where Putman included a small chapel on the northeast end of his addition.

In 1953 an alumna from the class of 1908 offered the college the funds for a real chapel. Her name was Helen Hills and she had married a cousin of the same name, becoming Helen Hills Hills—hence the unusual name of the chapel. Mrs. Hills was a staunch Congregationalist with very definite ideas about what she wanted her chapel to look like. When she offered her gift to the college she made it clear that she wanted it built in the style of the older New England churches from the late eighteenth and early nineteenth centuries, pointing to examples of Congregational churches in Norwalk, Connecticut, and Falmouth, Massachusetts as prototypes.

The college commissioned William and Geoffrey Platt of New York, who were already at work on Lamont House and had done extensive work at Deerfield Academy in a traditional redbrick neo-Georgian style. As the bene-factress wished, they designed Helen Hills Hills Chapel as a gracious replica of the old New England churches. In plan it consists of an open narthex or foyer that gives way to a large airy nave, which can seat up to six hundred. Balconies line both sides and the rear where the choir was to sit. A shallow arch, defined by Ionic pilasters, frames the semi-circular chancel where the services are conducted. The white wooden pews are capped with mahogany as are the banisters in the balconies. Fluted Ionic columns add a slender grace and support the upper levels. While a cross now hangs on the wall of the chancel, in the early planning stages Stephen Trowbridge Crary of the religion department recommended that all religious motifs be easily moved so as to accommodate services of other faiths.[1] This sensivity to other religions continues today as the needs of many different faiths are met. The basement included a bridal dressing room as it was understood that many Smith alumnae would want to be married here.

On the exterior the chapel is clad in white clapboards. A grand two-story entrance porch with Ionic columns and a pediment greet the visitor.

OPPOSITE: *Helen Hills Hills Chapel*

Helen Hills Hills Chapel, interior

The spire, decorated with classical details, rises from a square base with an ocular window, ending in a delicate point crowned by a weathervane. Wright was thrilled with the new chapel, writing to Mrs. Hills:

> College people and townspeople alike are already thinking of Helen Hills Hills Chapel as one of the landmarks of the city, as well as one of the most beautiful buildings in the vicinity. It will be remembered by many generations of Smith College students as one of the outstanding features of their college.[2]

The chapel has seen few changes since 1955. In 2002 the firm of Kuhn Riddle Architects added an elevator addition to the north end of the building in order to make it entirely accessible. This addition blends as seamlessly with the older structure as the chapel itself sits within a New England tradition of church architecture.

As we have seen, Smith College stressed domesticity in its student residences from the beginning, taking the family home as its model. Yet in the 1970s, many students began to ask for a different kind of domestic environment, one where they could live independently apart from the more structured house system with its head resident and house government. After President Neilson had worked so hard to house all Smith students on campus, some were now clamoring for the off-campus experience. This was a trend in colleges across the country. At Smith the result was the Friedman Complex, a series of townhouses that accommodate four students in each apartment, with separate bedrooms, a kitchen/dining area, living room, and bathroom.

Beginning in 1975, Smith was researching the idea of townhouses as a more independent alternative to dormitory life. Surveys had shown that many women were keen to try out apartment-style living and rather than see an exodus into apartments in town, the college decided to build their own with funds it received from Eugenie Friedman (class of 1947) and her husband Robert Friedman. After much deliberation, a site was chosen behind Helen Hills Hills Chapel between Henshaw Avenue and Round Hill Road.

The architects, Earl R. Flansburgh & Associates, had built up a reputation for school design throughout the 1970s, and the firm's work was featured in *Architectural Record*'s 1976 issue devoted to school architecture. Flansburgh went on to work with Hugh Stubbins in the 1980s, converting a series of old warehouses into Boston's Harborside Design

Friedman Complex

Center and more recently working to restore the Boott Cotton Mills Museum, which is part of the Lowell National Historic Park. These later works demanded a sensitivity to the historic fabric of a place. But in the 1970s this historicism was out of vogue and the ideals of the modern movement still held sway. For the Friedman Complex, Flansburgh relied on the solid, simple massing of his townhouses to complement the neighboring buildings. He wrote:

> Although these adjacent buildings are each of a different architectural style, they have simple massing in common and that salient architectural feature was selected as the inspiration for these Townhouses.[3]

Ironically, the houses' unornamented, boxy nature mark them clearly as a product of their time.

The Friedman Complex is made up of four distinct units, with two larger ones containing four apartments and two smaller ones that are made up of two apartments each. All are clad in vertical siding. The entrance facades have simple doors set beneath an overhanging second story. In some units long bands of casement windows light the upstairs bedrooms. Each unit has a dramatic dormer with clerestory windows, providing light for the staircases within and giving the buildings a jagged silhouette. On the back facades, simple casement windows light the second floor while sliding glass doors on the ground floor provide each unit with a second entry. A rhythm of solid and void is created by stepping each unit back from its neighbor, thereby clearly defining the townhouses and adding visual interest.

The units are still popular with students wishing to experience the independence of apartment life and they live up to President Jill Ker Conway's promise to Friedman in 1976:

> We think the design is elegant and that the new residential facility sited so imaginatively on the rising land between Henshaw Avenue and Round Hill Road will contribute a new and valuable aspect to student life at Smith.[4]

Parsons House

36. Parsons House *Architect unknown, 1902*

Renovation *Margo Jones, 1994*

Smith's proximity to two private girls' schools, the Burnham School and the Capen School, run by Bessie Capen, was benefical to the college in several ways. Many graduates of these schools went on to Smith for college, and when Capen died in February 1921, Smith was bequeathed the property of her school, which included three dormitories, a gymnasium, a classroom building, two cottages, and tennis courts. This was a large addition to the college and helped President Neilson in his efforts to house all of Smith's students on campus.

One of the dormitories acquired by Smith at this time was what is now called Parsons House, named for the Parsons family, one of the first families to settle in Northampton. (As part of the Capen School it was called Faunce Hall.) Built in 1902, the large rectangular block with a short ell stretching behind it to the north included a recitation hall and library. A central entrance porch, now enclosed, greets the visitor, while another large open porch on the west side, supported by Doric columns and crowned by a balustrade, makes a cool breezy refuge from the heat of late spring and early fall. The sheltering gambrel roof is interrupted by four shingled dormers and the whole is completed by a squat cupola.

In spite of its size, Parsons House fits in comfortably among its domestic neighbors with its use of clapboard on the second and third floors (above a brick first floor), shingle siding, cheerful dormer windows, and large porch. It was renovated in 1994 according to plans drawn up by Margo Jones and now has new energy-efficient windows, upgraded heating, plumbing, and safety systems, as well as new gutters and a slate roof. Like all of Smith's houses, it has its own traditions and rituals. One in particular happens on Halloween when residents dressed in costumes hand out candy in Neilson Library, sweetening a night of hard work for students who stayed in and studied.

37. Parsons Annex *Architect unknown, 1896*

Renovation *Kuhn Riddle Architects, 2001*

What is now Parsons Annex on Round Hill Road has been known by many different names since it was built in 1896. It was originally a private residence for the Walker family, who owned it until 1966 when it was briefly the property of the Burnham School. In 1968 Smith College purchased the site and the house became Parsons Annex. It changed its name again in 1977 to Hover House in honor of Edith Hopkins Hover (class of 1927), the founder of the Sophia Smith Associates Program, which helped raise money for the college from alumnae. As Hover House, it functioned as a co-op. It became Parsons Annex again in 1984, sharing meals, parties, and student government with Parsons House.

Parsons's calm and gracious exterior is made up of a square block whose surface is enlivened by a classical entrance porch and a large central gable above, lit by an attractive Palladian window. It has many aspects of the colonial revival, such as the symmetrical facade, clapboard siding, and shutters, as well as elements borrowed from the Queen Anne style, such as the delicate tracery in the oval window on the north side or the scalloped shingles around the dormers and the oriel windows.

Capen House

38. Capen House   *Thomas Pratt, 1825*

Addition *Architects unknown, 1885*

Addition *Architects unknown, 1891*

Renovations *Livermore and Edwards, 1995*

The historic buildings owned by Smith College help make the campus unique and offer a living classroom to students of American architecture. Capen House is representative of the popular Greek revival style of the early nineteenth century. It was built for Samuel Howe, an important figure in Northampton at the time and one of the founders of the Northampton Law School. In 1830 the house was purchased by the Talbot family from New York City, who used it as a summer home for many years. It remained in the Talbots' posession until 1883 when it was bought by Bessie T. Capen.

At a time when most women were still being tutored in embroidery and watercolors, Capen was an impressive exception. She was the second woman to be admitted to the Massachusetts Institute of Technology, from where she went on to teach chemistry at Wellesley College before coming to Smith in 1877. After her friend Mary Burnham, who had founded the Northampton Classical School for Girls in 1877 with Capen's help, died in 1885, Capen continued to run the school. By 1910 legal difficulties resulted in two schools, the Burnham School and the Capen School.

Capen had a close working relationship with presidents Seelye, Burton, and Neilson, and at her death in 1920 the property of the Capen

School came to Smith. It was a huge acquistion for the college, providing much needed dormitory space and a gymnasium.

Like the school, Capen House grew over the years. The original building of 1825 greets the visitor with grand two-story Ionic columns supporting a heavy entablature and pediment. The window in this pediment was added later, as were the two wings that stretch out behind the building to the north. These have clapboard siding and open porches over the entryways, giving the additions a less formal quality than that of the main facade. Large gables on both wings are tied to the original house by bold dentils that outline the pediments and entablatures. The effect of classical grandeur is heightened by its location on a small rise and by the full-length windows that light the ground floor.

A thorough renovation in 1995 replaced the roof and gutters, and upgraded the mechanical systems. It also completely refurbished the two wings, gutting the interiors and replacing old floors and windows. While now a much safer and warmer house for students, alumna Renee Landrum lamented the changes in an article she wrote for *Hampshire Life* in 1997, where she described the thrill of living in a house that was 170 years old and of a fondness she had for its eccentricities. She loved how the "wooden floors creaked underfoot, reminding us with every step that the house had a life of its own."[5] Yet in what has become a proud Smith tradition, much of the old fabric of the original Capen House was saved.

39. Davis Center *Architect unknown, 1898*

Renovation *Lukas Designs, 2004*

Alumnae from the past fifty years will remember the Davis Center as a place to meet friends, go to dances, catch a bite to eat, and meet to participate in the many student organizations on campus. Until 2004, when the new Campus Center opened, Davis was the hub of student life at Smith. The building began as a gymnasium for the Capen School. When Smith acquired the property in 1921, it continued to serve as a gymnasium to help with overflow from Alumnae Gym. After the Scott Gymnasium was built in 1924, Davis, then called Faunce Hall, housed the Department of Spoken English. In the 1920s and early 1930s, students were required to take a speech exam when they first entered college. If their acccents and pronunciation did not meet certain standards, students were encouraged to take locution lessons offered by the Department of Spoken English. This procedure had become unpopular by the mid-1930s and was abolished by President Neilson.

By 1942 Faunce Hall was one of several Smith buildings used by the Officer Training School for Women, but its military function lasted only two years before it became a much needed student center under the new name

Davis Center

Davis in honor of President Davis. Though it took several years to organize and furnish Davis as a successful student center, in 1949 it opened under the directorship of Mrs. A. C. Ockenden. She wrote in 1953 that Davis was the "hearthstone" of the campus and that

> the importance of leisure time cannot be overestimated, and a well-balanced program of extracurricular activities on campus is essential if our graduates are to be "educated for living" as well as for "making a living."[6]

Davis offered a food shop, offices for various campus organizations, as well as a large ballroom on the second floor, which was set up with ping pong tables, card tables, and intimate seating arrangements, all of which could be easily moved for large dances. The lounge could be reserved by students and was for women with dates only. In a brochure put out in 1950 by the Recreation Council, a body of students that ran the center together with Ockenden, discussed the offerings to be found in Davis and the importance of the center in the dating life of women. Under the subtitle "Just a Few Rules and Suggestions" the council warns:

> We have found over the years that the population of Northampton increases considerably over the weekends. Could this be due to Smith? Since we all enjoy the influx of men, here is something to remember. Neatness creates a favorable impression, therefore even dateless girls should look their best on Fridays, Saturdays, and Sundays. Why not let the men wear the pants on the weekends?[7]

By the 1950s the social life of Smith was dominated by mixers and an influx of male undergraduates from Havard, Yale, Dartmouth, and other men's colleges. Davis became an important focus for these events. Over the past fifty years the role of Davis did not alter much, though the nature of parties, dress, and behavior were revolutionized in the 1960s and 1970s. Since the opening of the new Campus Center in 2004, Davis is the home of the Mwangi Cultural Center (orginally in Lilly Hall). It also houses the offices of the Black Students Alliance (BSA), Nosotras, the Smith African Students Association (SASA), and the Asian Students Alliance (ASA).

While the building's function has changed since 1896, its appearance has not. It is still an elegant classical building, framed by entrances on both ends. The yellow clapboards of the second and third floors are punctuated by slender Ionic pilasters and large multipaned windows lighting what is still on occasion the ballroom. Twin copper-topped cupolas crown the hipped roof. While its classical details lend the building a formal balance, the relatively unobtrusive entryways give it an informality that is fitting to its changing roles as gymnasium, officer training building, student center, and now cultural center. It has both grandeur and accessibility as it continues to be an important feature on campus.

40. Cutter and Ziskind Houses

Skidmore, Owings & Merrill, 1957

Dining room addition *Leon Pernice & Associates, 1983*

To study the history of Cutter and Ziskind houses is to examine in microcosm the modern movement in architecture. All the controversy over the battle of styles, the struggle between form and function, and the tension between looking ahead and looking back is encapsulated in these two dormitories lining Elm Street.

Even after King and Scales houses were built and the great Quadrangle completed, Smith still struggled to house all of its students. In 1955, with a Board of Trustees interested in seeing something new and contemporary built on campus, plans were solicited by the firm of Skidmore, Owings & Merrill of New York for two new houses. One was to be named after Jacob Ziskind, an industrialist and philanthropist whose sisters had attended Smith and whose generosity made the dormitory possible. The other was named in honor of Elizabeth Reeve Cutter Morrow (class of 1896), who worked tirelessly for the college, beginning as the president of the Alumnae Association in 1917, then as a trustee; she was acting president of the college from 1939 to 1940 and chairman of the Board of Trustees from 1948 to 1950.

Drawings for the houses were published in the *Smith Alumnae Quarterly* in the spring of 1956. Even before this official unveiling, alumnae

Cutter and Ziskind Houses

clubs from around the country were writing to President Wright expressing concern about the modern style of architecture. In response, Wright sent a letter to the presidents of the Smith College clubs around the country, in which he argued that to build in a contemporary style was in keeping with a tradition at Smith that dated back to its founding when College Hall was built in the style of the day. Though he admitted that he too was wary of modern architecture, he and the trustees felt that the new dormitories would enhance the campus with their "grace and beauty."[8] Thus Cutter and Ziskind houses were built and opened in 1957.

Proponents of modern architecture saw beauty and honesty in the purity of the structure of modern buildings and embraced technologies that made that structure possible. In the hands of an architect like Mies van der Rohe such buildings are elegant examples of the union of modern materials and careful design. Gordon Bunshaft, the main architect of the Smith College project, was heavily influenced by Mies. But he and his firm were not known for their domestic work and many of their buildings from this time look very much alike, whether designed as office buildings, apartments, or dormitories. For example, the Karl Taylor Compton Laboratories, designed by Bunshaft for M.I.T. in Cambridge, Massachusetts, and opened the same year as Cutter and Ziskind, is strikingly similar in appearance. Containing classrooms, offices, and laboratories, the Compton building has a white skeletal grid that is exposed on the upper floors and rests on white piers set before recessed white brick walls and clerestory windows. The windows in the upper floors are the same as those found at Smith.

Certainly Cutter and Ziskind are not obviously domestic in nature. Each house is built in the shape of an ell, with the short, one-story arms united to form an inner courtyard that is closed along Elm Street by a white brick wall. The facades that front Henshaw and Prospect streets consist of long three-story white grids with large glass windows and aluminum mouldings floating above the brick walls and clerestory windows on the ground floor. The rectangular units within the grid identify each room and could stretch on indefinitely, either vertically or horizontally. Along Elm Street, gray brick infill provides closure to the street facade.

41. John M. Greene Hall   *Charles A. Rich, 1910*

Renovation *Francis W. Roudebush, 1947*

By the early twentieth century, the small-scale domestic nature of Smith was changing. The erection of Seelye Hall in 1898 heralded a new era of confident building for the college that included Neilson Library in 1909 and John M. Greene Hall, completed in 1910. This was the same year that President Seelye passed the oars of the college over to Marion L. Burton after more than thirty years at the helm. In 1911, during chapel services, President Burton announced that the new hall would be named for John M. Greene, a driving force behind the founding of the college. It was Greene, Sophia Smith's pastor in Hatfield, who advised her to consider a college for women.

Until Greene Hall was built, assemblies and daily chapel were held in the large Assembly Hall in College Hall. But by the turn of the century, this could no longer hold the student population and there was nowhere for the entire college to gather. As early as 1901, an anonymous donor had given funds for a large assembly hall. In 1906 the firm of Rand and Skinner, architects of Chapin House, had drawn up plans for such a hall, but a disagreement between them and the college led to the abandonment of the project. However, the need for a large hall was great and by 1909 construction of a building along Elm Street had begun. This time Charles A. Rich, who had just completed Baldwin House and was working on Northrop and Gillett houses, was commissioned. He would later also build Burton Hall (1914) for the college.

Rich had spent three years studying architecture in Europe, and for this important public building he looked back to the Roman and Renaissance traditions. Where Lord and Hewitt had employed a modest Renaissance style and red brick with red stone dressing for the library, Rich used the same materials and some of the same motifs with more architectural drama. At the main facade, huge Ionic columns of red sandstone support a weighty entablature and dentilled pediment. The scale alone harks back to ancient Rome, but the rose window set within the pediment is reminiscent of medieval church architecture. Three tall doors provide entry, with the one in the center highlighted by a curving pediment.

John M. Greene Hall

On the two side facades, semi-circular windows light the second floor of the nave, while ordinary sash windows are used throughout the rest of the building. The hall breaks out in a shallow curve at the western end. Both in scale and style the building asserts its importance in the life of the college and by fronting Elm Street it reaches out to the city as well.

The interior of Greene Hall underwent a major renovation in the 1940s. In 1943 President Davis discussed the problems of acoustics and lighting in the hall with architect Francis W. Roudebush. According to letters between Davis and Roudebush, the sound quality in the hall was very poor and "the horrible glare from the lights on the platform and particularly on the gilt organ pipes...is quite unbearable."[9] The solution, according to Roudebush, was to flatten the procenium arch by removing the "ugly"[10] moldings, to lower the ceiling and add new acoustical panels, to redesign the lighting, and to cover the organ and large side windows with a decorative geometric grid. These wooden grilles, which remain on the windows today, were designed to lessen the glare from the windows and help with acoustics. The resulting geometric rhythm, reminiscent of a painting by Piet Mondrian, is a modest precursor of modern architecure, which would arrive on campus ten years later with Cutter and Ziskind.

It is interesting to compare Greene Hall with its new neighbor, the Campus Center. Both provide a unifying focus for the college, but where the Campus Center was designed to be a place for casual interchange, Greene Hall is a place of assembly for chapel, inaugurations, anniversaries, and concerts. The grand formality of the facade reflects the role this building plays on campus. The relief of President Seelye on the south side of the entrance portico (by Alice Morgan Wright) watches students file past on their way to be entertained, instructed, and inspired.

42. Drew Hall, Career Development Office

Architect unknown, c. 1715

Located directly opposite the high modernism of Cutter and Ziskind houses is Elizabeth Drew Hall. Ironically, while Cutter and Ziskind in no way advertise their domestic nature, Drew Hall, so obviously a house, is home to the Career Development Office. Yet, it has had a long history as a residence. Built in the early eighteenth century by Benjamin Lyman, it remained in the Lyman family until the early nineteenth century, serving for a time as the parsonage for the Edwards Church.

Like many of its neighbors on Elm Street, it eventually became a boarding house for Smith College students. Between 1887 and 1899 it was known as Mrs. Tucker's after the owner, Lydia Tucker, who passed it on to her daughter, Abby, who continued the business. In 1929, after Miss Tucker's death, Edith Parker ran the house, which became known as the Brass Knocker. By this time it was less of a boarding house and more of an inn, offering meals and accommodation to those visiting Smith. In 1963 Smith purchased the property, first as a place for graduate students to live, then as a Senior House. It was named after Elizabeth Drew, who had been a lecturer at Girton College, Cambridge, before teaching at Smith. An author and poet, her work and lectures were much loved by the college community. In 1977 the building was renovated to serve as the Office of Admission. When Admission moved to Garrison Hall on West Street in 1985, Drew Hall became the Office of Career Development.

The brick exterior, simple symmetry, and slightly raised brick stringcourse of Smith's oldest building are reminiscent of early Georgian

Drew Hall

architecture in England, but the shutters add a decidedly American touch. The oversized dormers are from the late nineteenth or early twentieth centuries. A photo in the Smith College Archives from 1892 shows only the central dormer, which is treated with scalloped shingles above the window, a detail typical of the shingle style. The two later dormers are unusual with their two windows set at forty-five-degree angles to the wall surface, projecting forward like the bow of a ship. Perhaps due to its venerable age, or the formal use of brick, Drew Hall holds its own next to the new Campus Center, its quiet dignity calm beside its more jubilant neighbor.

43. Smith College Campus Center
Weiss/Manfredi Architects, 2003

While the house system is one of the most striking and popular features about Smith College, a task force, formed in 1996 to study the issue of a new campus center, found that it also fostered isolation and diminished the sense of community on campus. One of the many criteria put before the architects of the new Campus Center, Marion Weiss and Michael Manfredi, was to create a space that would lure students out of their houses and into a common area where they could eat, socialize, carry on a debate from class, or meet with their professors. The architects were also charged with the task of designing an attractive building that would not deprive the campus community of much loved green space. Further constrictions included a site beside a small power substation next to Drew Hall and the ever-present tension of designing a modern building along historic Elm Street.

The firm's first plans, which showed a large brick and glass building, were rejected by the Historic District Committee. In an interview Committee Chair Denis Nolan explained, "we just do not want another Cutter Ziskind."[11] In their revised design the architects shrunk the Elm Street facade and replaced the brick with wooden boards and battens stained white.

In addition to satisfying the Historic District Committee, Weiss and Manfredi carefully considered the campus as a whole and the site in particular, envisioning their building as growing "around a path rather than blocking a path or changing a path."[12] Indeed, as it snakes through the tight site between Drew Hall and Haven House, the center is reminiscent of the winding paths Smith's students travel every day.

The board-and-batten cladding has faint historical echos. Though no buildings on campus have this sort of cladding, it is a treatment used in the nineteenth century. The white certainly ties the building to its neighbors such as Cutter and Ziskind, Sessions House, and Helen Hills Hills Chapel. But the Campus Center does not recycle historical details in a postmodern manner. While nodding to the past, it moves forward boldly into the twenty-first century. The Elm Street facade is an angular union of two boxy units held together by a glass-covered atrium. Modest windows punctuate the wall surface, sometimes breaking out of the wall in an updated version of an oriel window. Upon entering from Elm Street, the polished cement path leads visitors past a curving wall of offices and computer terminals on the left and open stairs to the basement on the right, toward a wall of light. On this southern end, looking out over Chapin Lawn, the two units open up into great glazed walls that bathe the interiors in sunlight.

The Campus Center houses a popular café, above which is a large multi-purpose room and several lounges and offices for student

Campus Center

Campus Center, lounge

organizations. A lounge with a circular fireplace is opposite the café on the first floor, and behind it are more rooms that can be used for meetings and art exhibitions. While the effects of glass and steel dominate the interior, the use of color is also dramatic. Glimpses of red, green, blue, or purple are seen behind walls or through glass and help to define different spaces in the building.

The Campus Center has been warmly received by students and faculty alike. With the post office and bookstore in the basement level, as well as a game room, it has become a campus hub. It has been praised for the way it has integrated into the exisiting landscape of Smith and become its social core. It is an open building—open to students and staff as well as the town and the landscape. In the words of Clifford Pearson of the *Architectural Record*, "Instead of boundaries, they [the architects] created permeable membranes between indoors and out, campus and town, work and play."[13]

The firm of Weiss/Manfredi received the prestigious AIA Design Award in 2005 for their work at Smith. Both as an architectural feature and a social connector, the Campus Center has become a dynamic facet of life at Smith.

Addition *Architect unknown, between 1905 and 1916*

Renovations *Goody Clancy & Associates, 1996*

Sessions House is the second oldest building on campus after Drew Hall. As such it has a long and romantic history that continues to delight and attract students. While the records vary about its actual date, ranging from 1700 to 1751, the date of 1751, given by Megan Gardner in a paper she researched in collaboration with Smith College and Historic Deerfield, is the most recent and probably most accurate. It was built by Captain Jonathan Hunt, son of Deacon Johnathan Hunt, one of the founders of Northampton. At the time, the Georgian style of the house with its classical details and gambrel roof clearly advertised the family's wealth and prestige.

When Sessions was built, it was outside the protected area of Northampton. This left the family feeling vulnerable, and allegedly a secret staircase and passageway were built into the fabric to provide extra safety from the local Native Americans. This hidden stair and passage have ignited the imaginations of Sessions' many inhabitants over the years, who have enhanced the legends attached to it. One such story is set during the Revolutionary War, when the Hunt family hosted a prisoner, General John Burgoyne, who was captured after surrendering at the Battle of Saratoga in 1777. Legend has it that he and Hunt's daughter, Lucy, fell in love and had their romantic trysts in the secret passageway of the house. He later returned to England, and it is said that one or both of their ghosts still haunt the house (especially on Halloween). Students have reported seeing ghosts in Sessions, but whether these reports of the paranormal are true or not, renovations in 1996 did uncover evidence of a hidden space behind the central chimney that led down to the basement.

The house was a lively social residence in the nineteenth century. In 1900 Ruth Huntington Sessions bought it and opened it as an off-campus residence. At some point during her tenure a large addition was built behind the house. On old photographs from 1905 only a small wing is visible, but by 1916 photos show the long wing that still exists, stretching out harmoniously away from Elm Street. In 1921 the college bought the house and named it Sessions in honor of its previous owner. It was described by G. A. Borgese, professor of comparative literature, in the 1933 *Smith Alumnae Quarterly*:

> One of the oldest of the place, with its hiding places, and its fireplace almost as big as itself; still filled with the ghosts, ballads, and romantic loves of the late 18th century. Now it is the collective abode of a group of college students, and the Head, or Housemother, as these lay abbesses are called, in an attempt to subdue the youthful fire and the simultaneous chatter of her fifty daughters, has attached to the

Sessions House

architrave of the dining room the epitaph which disconsolate Lear decreed for Cordelia, "Her voice was ever soft, gentle and low, an excellent thing in a woman."[14]

Praise for such a quote and its placement in a Smith residence illustrate the tension present in women's colleges well into the twentieth century. The feminine paradigm was not easily shed despite women's gains in education.

In comparison with its exuberant Victorian neighbors along Elm Street and Helen Hills Hills Chapel next door, Sessions House, with its white clapboard siding, green shutters, and restrained classical entrance porch, seems modest and almost inconspicuous. It is easy to forget that such examples of early Georgian architecture are the basis for the many neo-Colonial houses built in the suburbs of America over the last hundred years. The addition, made when it was still a boarding house, increased the number of students Sessions could accommodate and probably made it practical for the college to buy the house in 1921. Its long and lively history and its significant eighteenth-century architecture, make it one of the college's most appealing houses.

45. Sessions Annex

Architect unknown, 1872

Addition and renovation *R. E. Dinneen Architects & Planners, 2001*

Sessions Annex

Where Sessions House exudes a symmetrical simplicity, its neighbor Sessions Annex is a picturesque pile with a varied silhouette and surface treatment typical of the Victorians. Built in 1872 for Edmund Pearson, who had come to Northampton from New Hampshire, it was not acquired by Smith until 1969. The house was a private residence until the 1920s when the owner, Mary Burgess, opened it as the White House Inn. Burgess offered to sell the house to Smith in 1921 and again in 1925, but on both occasions President Neilson declined. The subsequent owner, Louise van Dyke, sold it to Margaret Shakespeare, previously the Head of Haven and Wilder houses, in the 1950s, who ran the inn as "a resource for visiting alumnae, parents, and guests of Smith College, and a place of entertainment known for excellent food, gracious entertaining and memorable breakfasts."[15] After her death Ms. Shakespeare left it to Smith College. It was used for a time as a guest house and later as a male dormitory for men on the inter-college exchange. By the late 1970s it had become Sessions Annex.

The house has a large wrap-around porch and a square tower above the entrance that ends in a flat-topped pyramid. The contrasting red and gray tiles on the mansard roof with the diamond and square patterns are its most striking feature. Major renovations took place in 2001, including the addition of a wing on the back, an accessible entrance porch on the west, and internal upgrades. The porch and addition blend seamlessly with the older fabric of the house, carrying on the balustrade on the front and the corbels above the windows. Great care was taken to match materials and colors. The fire, heating, electrical, and plumbing systems were all upgraded to increase safety and comfort for residents.

Paradise Road

Elm Street

Round Hill Road

College Lane

Henshaw Avenue

Prospect Street

47a

47b

48

49

52

46a

56

51

50

46b

55

Bedford Terrace

57

54

53

58

Pond

Mary Ellen Chase House

46. Mary Ellen Chase House and Eleanor Duckett House

Chase House *Architect unknown, c. 1810*

Addition, Chase House *Probably William Fenno Pratt, Jr., 1879*

Addition, Chase House *William Fenno Pratt, Jr., 1880*

Duckett House *Architect unknown, c. 1810*

Dining hall addition *Duckett, Drummey Rosane Anderson Architects, 1974*

Connector between two houses *Juster Pope Frazier, 1995*

Kitchen renovations *LE & Associates, 1999*

Chase and Duckett houses have existed side by side for almost two hundred years. While their independent histories are rich and varied, they have been architecturally connected since 1973. An addition in 1995 made this connection more obvious and has further unified the two houses, which share clapboard siding and classical details. Both were built around 1810 on Elm Street as private residences but by the late nineteenth century they had taken on academic roles. From 1877 Chase House, then called Burnham House, served as the main residence for the Northampton Classical School for Girls founded by Bessie Capen and Mary Burnham (see page 111).

The early success of the school necessitated an addition to the rear, which included a dining room in the basement, "a general school room and three recitation rooms on the first floor, with a studio and rooms for the girls on the two floors above."[1] A year later Burnham hired Pratt to add a mansard roof to the original house and a central tower over the entrance, which has since been removed. It is likely that Pratt was responsible for both additions due to the similarity of the dormers and roofline.

The original house was a relatively simple colonial, enlivened by an elegant entrance porch supported on Ionic columns and a gracious Palladian window above. On either side two-story bay windows break out of the rectangular box. The mansard roof adds a third story, which is lit by quaint dormers with painted timber crossties. To the rear of the building a large porch shelters the doorway, which is crowned by a delicate, shallow fan-light. Many functions of the Burnham School were held here until its merger with the Stoneleigh School in Greenfield in 1968.

On the corner of Elm Street and Bedford Terrace sits Duckett House, which was built for the Clark family, who sold it to Mary L. Southwick in 1886. She opened it as a boarding house for Smith College students and ran it as such until 1918. It was owned by the Alumnae Association for three years before it was bought by the Burnham School in 1921. In 1968, when Smith purchased the house, the college named it after Eleanor Duckett, a professor of Latin and an important figure on campus for over thirty years.

Like Chase, Duckett has a small classical entrance porch and clap-board siding. A large gable with heavy dentil work faces Elm Street, while a tall, two-story portico supporting an iron balcony separates the second and third floors along Bedford Terrace. Duckett has also grown over the years, most notably in 1973 when an addition by the college added a dining room and a graduate dining room, and connected Chase and Duckett along the backsides of both buildings. The unobtrusive, one-story addition is distinguished from its neighbors by its casement windows and angular wall surfaces.

In 1995 the college hired the architectural firm of Juster Pope Frazier from nearby Shelburne Falls to add a four-story stair and elevator tower as well as a two-story dining room to replace the basement dining room in Chase. The addition subtly blends the two houses. The tall rectangular brick block angles away from the Duckett extension and gently turns to meet the southerly wing of Chase. The use of light brick helps to meld the two clap-board structures and its solid shaft is reminiscent of a chimney. Banks of many-paned windows light the new interior spaces and further tie the addition to its older neighbors. Set back from the street, the bolder elements of the new structure are softened by the traditional windows and wall surfaces, thereby making a contemporary statement without detracting from the historical fabric.

With the renovations of their kitchens in 1999, Chase and Duckett houses are in excellent condition and continue to comfortably house students and add architectural grace along Elm Street.

47. Northrop and Gillett Houses *Charles A. Rich, 1911*

Renovations *Juster Pope Frazier, 1994*

Northrop and Gillett houses, named for two of Smith's earliest trustees, Birdseye Grant Northrop and Edward Bates Gillett, opened as dormitories in 1911 just as Burton took over the presidency. Following on the heels of Neilson Library and John M. Greene Hall, their bold red brick classicism is part of the confident building campaign Smith pursued in the early twentieth century.

The elegant and restrained neo-Georgian style of these two houses, designed by Charles A. Rich, was very popular for women's colleges at the turn of the century. Radcliff's first purpose-built residence, Bertram Hall (1901), was designed like a large country residence in red brick with elegant classical details. Rich's work for Barnard also relied on the classical vocabulary, though on a less intimate scale. Northrop and Gillett are sheathed in a warm red brick, with classical quoins defining the corners. Each house is in the shape of an ell, with gabled ends pulled forward along Elm Street, adding variety and avoiding institutional repetition. The gables and cornice are articulated by heavy dentils, and dormer windows break up the roofline.

The facades along Elm Street have no doorways. Instead the visitor enters via a classical colonnade, which unites the two houses and shelters students passing between them. Benches line the covered passage and delicate fanlights and leaded glass surround the entries. The colonnade is one of the most interesting features of Northrop and Gillett. Until 1911 Smith's houses stood as independent units and students were exposed to the elements when passing between buildings. Here, the colonnade provides protection as well as unity. Barnard's first three buildings were also to have been united by a colonnade, a feature that was never actually built.[2]

Northrop and Gillett broke with the domestic tradition at Smith of central entries facing outward. This served to offset their size and prominence on Elm Street and focused the two houses inward toward each other. The entrances facing Lamont House are more dramatic. Here, both houses have large entrance porches above which rise elegant classical windows.

OPPOSITE: *Gillett House*

The curved central window of the third floor pushes into the gable for added effect.

The colonnade was completely rebuilt in 1994 when Juster Pope Frazier replaced the old foundations, railings, and colonnade, replicating the older version exactly. The houses were also renovated, with particular emphasis on upgrading the bathrooms and adding several more bedrooms.

48. Lamont House *William and Geoffrey Platt, 1955*

Addition *Livermore and Edwards, 1994*

By the 1950s Smith's need for a new dormitory was growing urgent. There had been an effort to build new student residences in 1946 when the Museum of Modern Art and the magazine *Pencil Points* sponsored an ill-fated competition. The long, drawn-out struggle to build the winning design ultimately failed, and the college took a step away from modern trends in architecture. In 1953 Smith's consulting architect, James Kellum Smith, recommended William and Geoffrey Platt as architects for the new dorm and for what was to become Helen Hills Hills Chapel. The Platt brothers had built extensively at Phillips Academy and Deerfield Academy in a traditional neo-Georgian style similar to that seen in Smith's Quad.

As correspondence began between President Wright and the architects, William Platt wrote to Wright about his visit to a recent, modern dorm, Lakeside (1951), at Mount Holyoke:

> Lakeside is a good dormitory in plan, orientation, site, etc. Treatment modern but somewhat stereotyped. General impression, cold and impersonal. It might be a hospital. Women's dormitories should be feminine.[3]

This quote speaks volumes about the Platts' attitudes toward both modern architecture and what were considered to be the needs of women. As the design process progressed, Henry Russell Hitchcock, professor of art history at Smith and one of modernism's strongest proponents at the college, voiced his disappointment:

> It would seem that the architects had based themselves too largely on work done here a quarter of a century ago. It occurs to me that it might be well to obtain from them a third study which would represent their own boldest thinking on the problem.[4]

The brothers responded ten days later, positing that the site, just below Northrop and Gillett houses along Prospect Street, dictated to a large degree their stylistic choice and that their building, in a simple

Lamont House

neo-Georgian dress, would provide "a sense of order" as was found in the Quadrangle.[5] They believed that

> The building should be economical to construct and maintain.... Further than this, a barracks-like or institutional building should be avoided, and it should have a friendly, domestic character.[6]

The architects prevailed, and Lamont House, named for Mrs. Thomas W. Lamont, née Corliss (class of 1893), was opened in 1955. The exterior is clad in a familiar red brick. The simple, blocky entrance porch is supported on square piers, which are elaborated with Ionic capitals. To the rear, the original dining and living rooms were housed in a one-story connector between the two shallow wings. A high-tech intercom system made communication easy and students were very pleased with the new typing room in the basement.

In 1994, as part of the dining consolidation program, a new dining room was added off the back of the house. Designed by Livermore and Edwards, this octagonal room is linked to the old house via a brick connector. The use of materials and many-paned windows ties the new to the old. This light-flooded jewel finally lends Lamont the boldness and drama that Hitchcock had asked for so many years ago.

Talbot House

49. Talbot House   *Richardson and Driver, 1909*

In Smith's constant quest for student housing, Bessie Capen's bequest in 1921 of her land and school buildings was a great boon. By 1912 Capen's school had split from the Burnham School and Capen had built two new dormitories and a gymnasium, which, together with her house, made up the Capen School. Over the years, Capen maintained a close relationship with Smith and sent many of her students to the college. Thus it was not surprising that her properties were passed on to Smith at her death in 1921.

One of the buildings that went to the college was Talbot House, named after the Talbot family who had owned the land for many years. Built in 1909 just across the street from Capen's own house, this dormitory was designed by the Boston firm of Richardson and Driver in an eclectic mixture of domestic styles. It is a very large brick and stucco building, with five stories set under a sheltering gambrel roof. Great paired gables interrupt the roof and add variety to the north and south fronts, while spacious porches provide entry and leisure space. White trim around the many windows, doors, and porches highlights these features.

While the fabric of the house has changed little over the years, the nature of the student body certainly has. Beginning as a dormitory for girls, it catered to the needs of young high-school students, before becoming a home to college students in 1922. In the 1950s Talbot residents revived a tradition called "Dainty Day," which was described by a news release of 1953:

Guided by a set of rules for General Conduct, each member of the House set out to "Be her natural self—Amiable, Amusing, Considerate, Delectable, Delicate, Enchanting, Fascinating, Prim and Proper, Ravishing..."; to "wear a dress, skirt, frilly blouse, etc.," at all times during the day, and lastly to "Be sprightly, trip lightly."[7]

The day ended with a handmade hat competition.

Forty years later, residents of Talbot were concerned with more serious affairs. In 1991, after a homophobic note was found in the house, residents formed a Diversity Management Board and Policy to combat all forms of discrimination. Their organized and thorough approach served as a model for other houses, which adopted Talbot's policy.

50. Smith College Campus School

Richardson and Driver, Boston, 1918

Laundry Building *Densmore & LeClear, Boston, 1922*

Renovations, connector *Dietz & Company, 1996*

President Seelye's support for Capen and Burnham when they established their Classical School for Girls was the start of Smith's involvement in secondary education and the beginning of a commitment to all levels of education that continues to this day. The Smith College Campus School, originally called the Smith College Day School, has been run by the college in conjunction with the Department of Education since 1927 and provides high-quality, progressive education for students from kindergarten through sixth grade.

Campus School

Among the buildings that went to the college after Capen's death was Gill Hall, the Capen School's assembly hall. Designed by the firm of Richardson and Driver, who were also responsible for nearby Talbot House, the stuccoed building has a large hall, which first greets the visitor from Prospect Street. Further down the hill a second entrance leads to the wing with classrooms and offices. Both parts of the building are sheltered under gambrel roofs. Large banks of windows provide plenty of light to the interiors and over each entrance delicate fanlights add interest. A small wing was added to the rear of the building, though the date of this is not known.

By the mid-1990s the school needed more space. Just to the east of Gill lay the old Smith College Laundry Building, built in 1922 by the architects Densmore & LeClear, who were responsible for several large urban buildings in Boston in the 1920s. It was decided to incorporate this spare and functional building into Gill Hall, thereby adding six new classrooms and an art room and storage space. The firm of Dietz and Co. was responsible for the renovation.

An entrance ramp at the front facade now leads the visitor into Gill Hall. This ramp blends graciously with the older building and incorporates what has become the school's symbol of interlocking semi-circles with a solid circle between them. This motif, resembling a stylized child with arms outstretched, symbolic of children's enthusiasm for learning, is found in relief along the wall of the ramp as well as in the addition. To the rear of the building, toward State Street, Dietz & Co. connected the Laundry Hall to Gill via a stair and elevator tower. Using a combination of brick and stucco, the firm united the two structures in a seamless and energetic addition. Just below the eaves of the stucco tower and curving brick connector runs the school's symbol in low relief. A blue-tiled stringcourse adds color and an element of whimsy to the whole.

Comfortable in its newly renovated home, the Campus School provides a place of learning, not only for the students enrolled but for Smith education majors and graduate students in the Department of Education.

51. Conway House *Thomas Douglas Architects, 2006*

Tucked behind Talbot and Lamont Houses is a new home for Ada Comstock Scholars and their families. Aspects of the ten-unit apartment building grew out of suggestions from Adas themselves such as the view of the outdoor play area from the public room. Built in stucco and brick with triple pane windows and extra insulation, it promises to be a warm and comfortable new residence.

LEFT: *Conway House*
RIGHT: *Morgan Hall*

52. Morgan Hall, Department of Education

Architect unknown, 1907–08

Renovations *Dietz & Co., 1997*

The Department of Education at Smith was founded in 1912. After many
years in cramped quarters in Gill Hall, the department is now housed in
Morgan Hall just next door. The college purchased this colonial-revival
house in 1936 with money bequeathed from Elizabeth Morrow Morgan, and
for twenty-five years it was home to the Elizabeth Morrow Morgan Nursery
School. In the 1960s, the nursery school was moved to its present building
on Fort Hill, which has improved playground facilities, and the Department
of Education moved into its new premises.

Morgan Hall was originally built by Elizabeth Porter Cooper for
herself and her daughters. It is a white clapboard house with a central doorway under a classical porch and symmetrical windows on either side. The
shutters on the ground floor feature cut-out hearts, a charming detail that
would have been a welcoming touch for children enrolled in the preschool.
The 1997 renovation by Dietz & Co focused primarily on upgrading the
mechanical and electrical systems in the house, providing accessibility, and
reconfiguring the ground floor to better serve the needs of the education
department.

Baldwin House

Baldwin House was the first building for Smith designed by Charles A. Rich, who was well known for his collegiate architecture, designing the first buildings for Barnard College in the early years of the twentieth century and going on to work at Smith, Williams, Dartmouth, and Amherst. His other buildings at Smith include John M. Greene Hall, Northrop and Gillett houses, and Burton Hall.

Baldwin was named in honor of William H. Baldwin, Jr., who had been a trustee of the college from 1898 to 1905, and his wife, Ruth Bowles Baldwin (class of 1887), who worked as secretary to Seelye, as alumnae trustee from 1906 to 1912, and as a trustee from 1912 to 1932.

Sitting beside Albright House with its exuberant Queen Anne and half-timber details, the neo-Georgian Baldwin looks sedate and refined. Yet the red and black brick checkerboard pattern in which it is clad gives its wall surface a lively energy and the great curving entrance porch warmly welcomes the visitor. It is a large building, housing some seventy students in singles, doubles, and suites, but the classical details add variety and the bow windows on the ground floor as well as the dormers on the fourth lend the house a warm domesticity. Originally, the windows had shutters, which together with the delicate fanlights above the door and side windows, hark back to an American colonial tradition.

The large porch with its gentle curve rests on elaborate versions of Ionic columns. It was and still is a popular meeting place, furnished with chairs and a swing. Among Baldwin residents' traditions is their May Day celebration, when sleepy seniors are woken up at 5:30 a.m. to the sounds of freshmen "banging cooking utensils, singing a 'good morning song' and serving the seniors breakfast.... They all seem to love it, ... because it truly exhibits the friendliness and family-like atmosphere that forms in Baldwin."[8]

54. Albright House *William C. Brocklesby, 1900*

Albright House was the first Smith residence to be built on Bedford Terrace, which has since become an important link between the college and the town. It was named for John Joseph Albright of Buffalo, New York, who was an important supporter of Smith and the founder of the Albright Art Gallery in his hometown. His wife, Susan Gertrude Fuller, had graduated from Smith in 1891 and was an alumnae trustee from 1912 to 1918.

In his design for Albright House Brocklesby combined the lively Queen Anne style with a bold half-timber treatment that comes from the Old English style—an effort to recreate the look of an old English manor house. The street facade is of red brick with curving Flemish gables on both ends. The curves of the gables are echoed in the curving window frames in all but the basement windows and are particularly pronounced in the two-story insets framing the windows in the gable ends. Oriel windows dramatize the third floor and rounded dormers punctuate the roofline. Particular to the American Queen Anne were the shutters that once framed the windows and the large entrance porch. But seen from the front, Albright House bears a strong resemblance to Old Hall at Newnham College, Cambridge, designed by Basil Champneys in 1875. On the eastern and western ends of the building, Brocklesby boldly decorated the gables with a half-timber treatment of patterned wood against a stucco background, which adds interest and variety, capturing the visitor's attention from either end of Bedford Terrace.

By 1900 in England the Queen Anne and Old English styles were beginning to give way to the more staid neo-Georgian. Similarly, the next house built at Smith was Chapin House, which introduced classical elements in a more formal way.

Albright House

Dawes House

55. Dawes House *Architect unknown, c. 1890*

Dawes House has a complicated history. Now located at number 8 Bedford Terrace, for many years it was on Henshaw Avenue in what was originally home to the Quimby family. The Quimbys had run the house as an off-campus residence for Smith students until the college acquired the property in 1926 and named it for Anna L. Dawes. Dawes did not attend Smith but was an ardent supporter of women's higher education and one of the first women to be elected to the Board of Trustees in 1889 by Smith alumnae. During World War II, when students could no longer travel to France for their junior year abroad, Dawes became the French House on campus. Under the leadership of Jeanne Saleil, professor of French, it was a lively and vibrant house where students were immersed in French language and culture. By the 1970s this vibrancy had ebbed, and when space was needed for the new Friedman Complex, the house was razed.

Dawes House then moved to its present location at 8 Bedford Terrace into a house that was originally built for Dr. Mary Brewster, then Smith's physician. In 1913 the house was sold to Mary Lois James, who opened it as an Alumnae House and tearoom, which she ran until 1922. The college bought it in 1935 and it continued to house the Alumnae Association until 1938, when their new building was opened. In the years between 1935 and 1977, it served a variety of functions before it became the French House.

The original house was a simple colonial revival with a gambrel roof and delicate details such as the curving pediment in the central dormer and the fanlight over the entry beneath a porch supported by Doric columns. Ornate capitals on pilasters frame the corners of the house. At some point a room was added above the front porch and a small wing enlarged the house on the western corner. In what has become characteristic of Smith, this sub-dued, yet elegant residence has been refitted to adapt to the ever-changing needs of the college community, its stable exterior belying its many roles and the active life within.

56. Unity House *Architect unknown, 1880*

Renovation *Thomas Douglas Architects, 1999*

What is now Unity House was built in 1880 for the Burnham School, provid-ing a laboratory and lecture rooms. It was used for these purposes until 1968 when the college acquired the Burnham School property and renovated the building for use as a space for students living off campus to meet and study. Students who commuted to college were originally known as the Luba Club, with Luba standing for "Let Us Be Acquainted." The club was founded in 1920 to give those students a sense of community when on campus and had many different homes over the years, ranging from a room in the Students' Building to space in the basement of Albright. Its name was changed in 1946 to Hampshire House, a name that indicated its members' ties to Hampshire County while offering some elements of the house system for these local students.

When the college renovated the building in 1969, students had some say in its requirements, and it was outfitted with a kitchen, a large liv-ing room, a study room, and two bathrooms.[9] As Hampshire House, the building offered students who lived at home an important means of con-necting with the social life on campus. In 1990 the club moved to office space in the old college bookstore on Green Street, and its former residence

Unity House

was renamed Carriage House. When organizations such as the Asian Students Association, the Black Students Alliance and the International Students Organization united to request a multicultural center where their members could relax and socialize, the Carriage House was designated as a shared space. The student leaders later changed the building's name to Unity House, "as a symbol of their togetherness and cooperation."[10]

    Unity House sits back from Bedford Terrace behind a parking lot. Its bright red brick stands out amidst its clapboard neighbors. On the right side of the house the curving brick frames around the windows are articulated by an alternating pattern of black and red bricks, a detail that is missing on the right side of the house, suggesting that perhaps it served a different purpose. There is a vague sense of symmetry to the building with two gables framing the center block but the western block protrudes from the wall whereas the eastern gable stays flush. Most dramatic are the large, multi-paned windows on the ground floor.

    Local architect Thomas Douglas renovated Unity House in 1999, upgrading the bathroom and adding two new kitchenettes as well as new workstations. Unity House continues to be the organizing hub of multicultural affairs at Smith, enriching the social and intellectual life of the college.

Alumnae House, living room

57. Alumnae House *Frederick J. Woodbridge, 1938*

For many years the varied activities of Smith alumnae were carried out in cramped offices in College Hall. In 1931 the Board of Trustees donated a plot of land on the corner of Elm Street and Bedford Terrace, the site of the old Tenney House, and the association began the process of raising funds for a building of their own.

The Alumnae Building Committee, consisting of Dorothy Zinsser (class of 1913), Elizabeth Morrow (class of 1896), Lucia Valentine (class of 1923), and Elizabeth Bryan (class of 1909), worked tirelessly over the next six years to carefully establish the building's requirements and to select an architect who could design a beautiful and functional building on a limited budget. The result would be one of Smith's most elegant buildings, designed by Frederick J. Woodbridge, an architect from the firm of Evans, Moore and Woodbridge of New York, whose mother and sister had attended Smith.

Built of brick and painted white, Alumnae House has offices on the southeast corner, located closest to College Hall, a terrace and lounge to the rear of the building, and a conference room on the corner of Bedford Terrace and Elm Street. This room has separate access and is connected to the office block via a gallery. The office block is the more domestic wing, with windows that have black shutters, a Grecian stringcourse dividing the first floor from the second, and dormer windows lighting the third floor. The entrance off of Bedford Terrace is under a pediment supported by squat Doric

TOP: *Alumnae House*
BOTTOM: *Alumnae House, dining room*

columns in the Greek revival style. The effect of the exterior is calm and restrained, dramatized by the Greek forms and stark white brick.

Inside there is a similar combination of clean modern forms with familiar decorative details. Around the entrance to the office block stylized fluted columns and a pediment surround the doorway, whereas in the large airy foyer, staircase, and gallery, Woodbridge's use of materials such as brass, glass, and a prima verra veneer provide stylish and polished spaces without the use of ornament. The highly reflective floor tiles, natural light, and contrast of materials create an elegant interior space unique at Smith. The gallery, where art by Smith alumnae sometimes hangs, leads to the conference room. Over each door attached columns support carved pediments with decorative details symbolic of women's search for knowledge at Smith. The lounge looks out over the Pelham Hills and opens out onto the terrace. Graceful curving stairs lead down to what is now known as Trudy's Garden, named for Gertrude Ridgway Stella (class of 1937), who was executive director of the Alumnae Association for many years.

Alumnae House should be enjoyed slowly to appreciate the many details that make it such an exciting building. These include the paving stone at the entrance, which is carved with a symbolic elm tree; the mural of the United States in the main office; and the whimsically painted lockers in the basement, which hold the belongings of each class. Alumnae House was designed to be a home to past students, a base to welcome them. It continues to function as such, providing formal elegant spaces and playful reminders of the women's days at college. When it was built, it served as an architectural link between the historical Greek style and the modern movement. In the words of the *Architectural Forum* of 1939, it provided "evidence that, in the hands of uninhibited designers, there is in the familiar vernacular no bar whatever to a restatement of tried and tested forms in convincing and contemporary terms."[11]

Stoddard Hall

58. Stoddard Hall and Annex *Herts and Tallant, 1899*

Stoddard Annex *Taylor and Putnam, 1919*

Renovations *Juster Pope Frazier, 1984–86*

Connector *Goody Clancy Architects, 1996*

The building of Stoddard Hall is a testament to the vitality and importance of the sciences at Smith even in its early years. In his report to the trustees in 1897 Seelye expressed concern about the overcrowded accommodations of the sciences, which were all crammed into Lilly Hall. He was hopeful that the construction of a chemistry building would relieve at least some of the pressure. By 1899 he could inform the trustees that the new chemistry building was a success both

> for personal comfort and scientific investigation. It gives also opportunity for courses of study in the application of chemistry to sanitation and food, which have not hitherto been open to students for lack of room, and which, it is hoped, will be found of much practical benefit in future life.[12]

This quote is significant not only for the importance that Seelye placed on the teaching of chemistry, but also within the context of the Social Darwinist movement. Social Darwinism posited that the education of women was vital to the future and health of the race and that educated women would be better able to raise strong and healthy children. Seelye and the trustees believed that the teaching of chemistry in college would be of great use to women as they set up their own homes.

Stoddard Hall, named in 1919 for John Tappan Stoddard, professor of chemistry at Smith for over forty years, was opened in early 1899. It was designed by the New York firm of Herts and Tallant, whose practice specialized in theater buildings, especially around Broadway in New York. Smith's chemistry building was one of their earliest commissions. The building faces Elm Street just beside Alumnae House. The elaborate lettering in the terra-cotta relief and the allegorical figures of Metallurgy and Alchemy that flank it, together with the heavily timbered entrance porch to the south, are clearly inspired by the Gothic revival of the earlier part of the nineteenth century. The building's tall red brick facade with brownstone dressing makes a powerful statement along Elm Street.

By 1918 there were calls from the department for an addition to the building to include three more large laboratories as well as smaller offices. Chemistry had become a very popular science, in large part because job opportunities were good for women graduates. In 1919 Stoddard Annex was built according to plans by Taylor and Putnam of Northampton. Located on the hillside behind Stoddard, only the second floor of the annex lined up exactly with the existing building. Small flights of stairs connected the two buildings, which are now quite separate and accessible to each other through the basement only. The architects used the same red brick of Stoddard Hall for their addition, but limited funds kept the design very simple.

The building of the large Clark Science Center made Stoddard Hall redundant as a chemistry building and it was vacated in 1967. A year later the art department made it their temporary home while the new art complex was completed, abandoning the building in 1972 for their new premises. Ironically, at a college where space has always been a premium, Stoddard Hall remained empty for over ten years while the college determined what best to use it for. In 1984 it was finally decided to house the computer science department here. The renovations, done by the architectural firm of Juster Pope Frazier, included an elevator and new staircase housed in an addition of brick and glass on the north side as well as many interior changes to accommodate late-twentieth-century technology. In the tradition of Smith's renovations, interior details such as the great brick mantelpiece in the first-floor office and the dramatic cantilevered staircase and oak trim remain.

The most recent addition to the Stoddard complex is a connector between the basement of Alumnae House and Stoddard Annex, designed by Goody Clancy Architects in 1996. On the Elm Street side the connector is faced in slate like a sleek garden wall. On the other side glass walls provide views of the Pelham Hills and the town of Northampton; curving stairs lead down to Trudy's Garden and Albright House. It is a subtle and quiet addition, which unites these two very different buildings. Stoddard Hall now houses Information Technology Services. The Office of Advancement, closely associated with the Alumnae Association, is found in Stoddard Annex.

Paradise Pond

Notes

Introduction

1. Sophia Smith, quoted in L. Clark Seelye, *The Early History of Smith College 1871–1910* (Boston and New York: Houghton Mifflin Co., 1923), 5.
2. Ibid., 20–21.
3. See Helen Lefkowitz Horowitz, *Alma Mater: Design and Experience in the Women's Colleges from Their Nineteenth-Century Beginnings to the 1930s*, 2nd ed. (Amherst, MA: University of Massachusetts Press, 1993): 73–75.
4. Seelye, *The Early History*, 20–21.
5. Basil Champneys, "The Planning of Collegiate Buildings." *Journal of the Royal Institute of British Architects* 10, 3rd series (1903): 205–12.
6. John Nolan, "Report and General Plans for the Re-arrangement of the Present Campus and the Extension of Smith College, Northampton MA" (1915), Burton Papers, Box 9, Smith College Archives (SCA).
7. "The Dedication of the Memorial to the Smith College Relief Unit," *Smith Alumnae Quarterly*, vol. 16, no. 1 (Nov. 1924): 115–16.
8. Ada L. Comstock, "Why Smith Should House Its Students" *Smith Alumnae Quarterly*, vol. II (Nov. 1919): 17.
9. "Report of the Jury," *Pencil Points* (April 1946): 52.
10. Lucia Valentine to Herbert Davis, May 1946, Davis Papers, Box 2, SCA.
11. Valentine to Davis, May 29, 1946, Davis Papers, Box 2, SCA.
12. Ibid., 3.
13. Yvonne Freccero to Otis B. Robinson of Shepley, Bulfinch, Richardson and Abbott, Oct. 4, 1985, Mary Maples Dunn Papers, Buildings and Grounds, Box 1, SCA.
14. Eric Sean Weld, "Working Toward a Sustainable Campus," *NewsSmith* (Fall 2005): 6.

An Academic Landscape

1. Mark Francis and Randolph T. Hester, eds., *The Meaning of Gardens* (Cambridge, MA and London: MIT, 1990): 4. This quotation is taken from their introductory essay "The Garden as Idea, Place and Action."
2. See Helen Horowitz, *Alma Mater: Design and Experience in the Women's Colleges From Their Nineteenth Century Beginnings to the 1930s* (New York: A. A. Knopf, 1984).
3. Report of the Alumnae Council of Smith College, Northampton, February 14–16, 1924. Smith College Alumnae Association Records, Alumnae Council Files, Box 3141. College Archivist Nanci Young discovered and called my attention to this passage.
4. Renowned architectural historian and Alice Pratt Brown Professor Emeritus of Art, Helen Searing details this in her essay "A History of the Art Buildings at Smith College," in *Image and Word: Art and Art History at Smith College* (Northampton: Smith College, 2003), 43–54.
5. James S. Polshek and Susan T. Rodriguez, "The Brown Fine Arts Center: An Architecture of Transformation," in *Image and Word*, 3.
6. C. John Burk, *Celebrating a Century: The Botanic Garden of Smith College* (Northampton: Smith College, 1995). Professor Burk also authored *The Gardens and Botanical Facilities of Smith College: Education, Research, and Pleasure* (Northampton: Smith College, 1981). Both are currently in print and have proven classics in their descriptions and analysis in all matters relating to the botanic garden.
7. Shavaun Towers and Cornelia Hahn Oberlander, *Smith College Landscape Master Plan* (Northampton: Smith College, 1995): Introduction.
8. Mary Maples Dunn, President of Smith College, "Landscape Mission Statement," 19 June 1995, in *Smith College Landscape Master Plan*. She argued for a master plan because "Over the years we have intruded into the original composition of the campus by building new structures, adding on to old structures and taking down standing structures. It is therefore time to arrive at a fresh understanding of our landscape, to explore the potential for enhancing the aesthetic, educational, intellectual and communal values of living on this campus.... And because change is constant we must seek a plan which allows us agility and flexibility."
9. For more about the Landscape Studies Program, visit www.smith.edu/landscapestudies.

10. For a complete history and descriptions of, and visitor information for, the botanic gardens, see http://www.smith.edu/garden.

11. Madelaine Zadik, "Another Side of William Frances Ganong," *Botanic Garden News* (Fall 2005): 14.

12. Beth Py-Lieberman, "Twigman Cometh," *Smithsonian* v. 31: no. 9 (Dec. 2000): 124.

13. Humphry Repton, "Sketches and Hints" (1795) in J. C. Loudon, *The Landscape Gardening and Landscape Architecture of the Late Humphry Repton, Esq.* (London and Edinburgh: Longman & Co. and A. C. Black, 1840), 52.

Walk One

1. See the original plans by Peabody & Stearns, 1875, Physical Plant, Smith College.

2. L. Clark Seelye, "Inaugural Address," *Addresses at the Inauguration of Rev. L. Clark Seelye as President of Smith College, and at the Dedication of Its Academic Building, July 14, 1875,* (Springfield MA: Clark W. Bryan & Co. 1875), 28.

3. Ester Wyman, "College Hall: History" (1966) Buildings and Grounds, College Hall, Box 16, 2, SCA.

4. Sarah Tiedeman, "College Hall: Architectural Report" (1949), Buildings and Grounds, College Hall, Box 16, SCA.

5. Eleanor Terry Lincoln and John Abel Pinto, *This, the House We Live In: The Smith College Campus from 1871 to 1982* (Northampton, MA: Smith College, 1983): 44.

6. Ibid., 44.

7. Philip Sawyer, "Early Days of York and Sawyer," in *Journal of the American Institute of Architects* 16 (November 1951): 197.

8. William Gillen, conversation with the author, December 7, 2004.

9. Ibid.

10. "Welcome to Hubbard House" (1959), Buildings and Grounds, Hubbard House, Box 40, SCA.

11. Barbara Sabo, "The Student's Handbook," (1961) Buildings and Grounds, Washburn House, Box 112, 11, SCA.

12. W. L. Stoddard, "Smith's New Library," *Boston Transcript* (Dec. 15, 1909), Buildings and Grounds, Neilson Library, Box 62, SCA.

13. Phoebe Taylor, "Men's Lodgings," *The Sophian* (November 6, 1969): 4. Buildings and Grounds, Alumnae Gymnasium, Box 34, SCA.

14. Thomas Mendenhall, memorandum to the Board of Trustees, September 23, 1959, Mendenhall Papers, Buildings and Grounds, Wright Hall, Box 6, SCA.

15. Horowitz, *Alma Mater*, 75.

16. Mary Breese Fuller, "Some Reminiscences," *Smith Alumnae Quarterly*, vol. 18, no. 1 (November 1926): 69.

17. Seelye, *Early History of Smith College*, 39.

18. "Dewey House Converted, Oak Closed," *Smith Alumnae Quarterly*, vol. 82, no. 4 (Fall 1998): 8.

19. Helen Searing, professor emeritus of Art History, e-mail to author, December 9, 2004.

20. Helen Searing, "A History of the Art Buildings at Smith College," *Image and Word: Art and Art History at Smith College* (Northampton, MA: Smith College, 2003): 23.

Walk Two

1. "Lawrence House and Its Self-Help Girls" in *The Girls' Companion* (Jan. 4, 1913), Buildings and Grounds, Lawrence House, Box 51, SCA.

2. New Student's Handbook (1987), Buildings and Grounds, Morris House, Box 80.

3. Thomas Mendenhall to Helge Westermann, 23 December, 1963, Mendenhall Papers, Buildings and Grounds, Box 5, SCA.

4. "New Buildings at Smith College: Plans for Gymnasium and Attractive Music Hall will be Ready in the Fall of 1924" (May 22, 1923), Buildings and Grounds, Scott Gymnasium, Box 35, SCA.

5. "Two New Buildings Finished at Smith," *Springfield Sunday Republican* (October 5, 1924), Buildings and Grounds, Sage Hall, Box 102, SCA.

6. Piper Wentz, "Improvement recommended for scandalous gym facilities" *The Sophian* (Oct. 11, 1973): 8, Buildings and Grounds, Ainsworth Gymnasium, Box 35, SCA.

7. Champneys, "The Planning of Collegiate Buildings," 205–12.

8. For more about Girton and Newnham see Margaret Birney Vickery, *Buildings for Bluestockings: The Architecture and Social History of Women's Colleges in Late Victorian Britain* (Newark: University of Delaware Press; London: Associated University Press, 1999).

9. "New Smith College Dormitory: Commodious Building Now Being Erected on the Campus at Northampton" (n.d.), Buildings and Grounds, Tyler House, Box 110, SCA.

10. "Brochure" (Dec. 1905), Buildings and Grounds, Burton Hall, Box 4: 1–2, SCA.

11. Joseph Richardson to Thomas Mendenhall, 28 July, 1961, Mendenhall Papers, Box 2, SCA.

12. Lincoln and Pinto, *This, the House We Live In*, 171.

13. Helen Searing to Mary Maples Dunn, October, 12, 1987, Mary Maples Dunn Papers, Box 1, SCA.

Walk Three

1. "Residence of President Neilson of Smith College," *House Beautiful* (June 1921): 482–83, Buildings and Grounds, President's House, Box 100, SCA.

2. Horowitz, *Alma Mater*, 309.

3. J. W. Ames and E. S. Dodge, "Report of Meeting at Smith College," Dec. 5, 1934, Neilson Papers, Box 44, SCA.

4. Lincoln and Pinto, *This, The House We Live In*, 126.

5. Mary Ellen Chase, "Invitation," c. 1954, Buildings and Grounds, Mason Infirmary, Box 43, SCA.

6. Katharine S. Stebbins, "The History of Park House 1924–25," Buildings and Grounds, Box 97.

7. Unidentified alumna, Buildings and Grounds, Hopkins House, Box 39, SCA.

8. Lincoln and Pinto, *This, The House We Live In*, 60.

9. David Handlin conversation with the author, January 27, 2006.

Walk Four

1. Stephen Trowbridge Crary, "Comments on Plans for Chapel," January 5, 1954, Wright Papers, Buildings and Grounds, Box 3, SCA.

2. June H. Fifield, "Congregationalist gives college chapel," *Advance* (April 6, 1955): 7, Buildings and Grounds, Helen Hills Hills Chapel, Box 9, SCA.

3. Earl Flansburgh, "Description of the residential Facility for Smith College located Between Henshaw Avenue and Round Hill Road," Conway Papers, Box 4, SCA.

4. Jill Ker Conway to Mrs. Robert Friedman, Nov. 12, 1976, Conway Files, Buildings and Grounds, Box 4, SCA.

5. Renee Landrum, "The Heart of a Home: A Makeover Robs a Dormitory of Some of Its Character—and Its Charm," *Hampshire Life*, (Jan. 27, 1997), Buildings and Grounds, Capen House, Box 5.

6. Mrs. A. C. Ockenden, "Davis Student Recreation Center, Smith College," Nov. 3, 1953, revised September 15, 1954, Buildings and Grounds, Davis Student Center, Box 22, SCA.

7. Recreation Council, "Davis Student Center," circa 1950, Buildings and Grounds, Davis Student Center, Box 22, SCA.

8. President Benjamin Wright to presidents of Smith College Alumnae Clubs, January 23, 1956, Buildings and Grounds, Cutter and Ziskind Houses, Box 20, SCA.

9. President Davis to Francis Roudebush, March 7, 1944, Davis Papers, Box 3, SCA.

10. Francis Wilshire Roudebush to President Herbert Davis, February 8, 1945, Davis Papers, Box 3, SCA.

11. "New Building for Smith College," *Daily Hampshire Gazette* (Jan. 13, 2000), Buildings and Grounds, Campus Center, Box 5, SCA.

12. Rachell Millman, "A Building grows out of a path," *The Sophian* (May 15, 2003): 3.

13. Clifford A. Pearson, "Weiss/Manfredi Integrate the Modern Smith College Campus Center into Its Historic and Natural Setting," *Architectural Record*, vol. 192, no. 8 (Aug 2004): 114.

14. G. A. Borgese, "Idyll of Northampton," *Smith Alumnae Quarterly*, vol. XXIV, no. 4 (Aug. 1933): 358, Buildings and Grounds, Box 105, SCA.

15. Lincoln and Pinto, *This, The House We Live In*, 180.

Walk Five

1. Miss Bessie Capen, *Address of Miss Capen at the 35th Reunion of the Capen School*, June 1912, published by the Capen School Association, 6.

2. Horowitz, *Alma Mater*, 139.

3. William Platt to President Wright, Nov. 9, 1953, Wright Papers, Buildings and Grounds, Box 3, SCA.

4. H. R. Hitchcock to President Wright, Jan. 10, 1954, Wright Papers, Buildings and Grounds, Box 3, SCA.

5. Geoffrey Platt to President Wright, Jan. 20, 1954, Wright Papers, Box 3, SCA.

6. Ibid.

7. "News Release of Student Activities" (1953), Buildings and Grounds, Talbot House, Box 108, SCA.

8. Lindsay Berger, "HONS packet to new students" (July 24, 1999), Buildings and Grounds, Baldwin House, Box 3, SCA.

9. "Local Girls Make Good at Smith: Campus Facility Honors County," *Daily Hampshire Gazette* (January 29, 1969), Buildings and Grounds, Hampshire House, Box 36, SCA.

10. "Unity House: A Safe Haven on Campus," *Acamedia* (Feb. 17, 2000), Buildings and Grounds, Unity House, Box 110, SCA.

11. "Alumnae House, Smith College, Northampton, MA," *Architectural Forum* (Jan. 1939), Buildings and Grounds, Alumnae House, Box 2, SCA.

12. L. Clark Seelye, *Annual Report of the President of Smith College, 1898–1899*, (Northampton, MA: Smith College, 1899): 24.

Bibliography

Collections
Physical Plant, drawings and plans, Smith College, Northampton, Massachusetts.
Smith College Archives, Smith College Library, Smith College, Northampton, Massachusetts.
Society for the Preservation of New England Antiquities, Boston, Massachusetts.

Smith College Periodicals
NewsSmith
Smith Alumnae Quarterly
The Sophian

"Alumnae House, Smith College, Northampton Mass." *Architectural Forum.* (Jan. 1939).
Barrett, Sarah Curran. "Family Riches" *Smith Alumnae Quarterly,* vol. LXXXVII, no. 1,(Winter 1995–1996):14.
Capen, Miss Bessie. *Address of Miss Capen at the 35th Reunion of the Capen School.* Northampton MA: Capen School Association, June 1912.
Champneys, Basil, "The Planning of Collegiate Buildings." *Journal of the Royal Institute of British Architects* 10, 3rd series. (1903): 205–12.
Clarke, Jessica, "Students work for diversity: Bias fought at Smith College." *Sunday Republican.* (Feb. 7, 1993).
Conway, Jill Ker. "Inaugural Address" *Smith Alumnae Quarterly,* vol. LXVII, no. 1, (Nov. 1975): 6–8.
Davis, J. Herbert. "Inaugural Address." *Smith Alumnae Quarterly* no. 32, (1940–1941): 3–6.
"Dewey House Converted, Oak Closed" *Smith Alumnae Quarterly,* vol. LXXXII, no. 4, (Fall 1991): 8.
Fuller, Mary Breese, "Some Reminiscences" *Smith Alumnae Quarterly* (Nov. 1926): 68–69.
Girouard, Mark. *Sweetness and Light.* New Haven: Yale University Press, 1977.
Hanscom, Elizabeth Deering and Helen French Greene. *Sophia Smith and the Beginnings of Smith College; based upon the narrative of John Mortimer Greene,* Northampton MA: Smith College, 1925.
Horowitz, Helen Lefkowitz, *Alma Mater: Design and Experience in the Women's Colleges from their Nineteenth-Century Beginnings to the 1930s.* 2nd, ed. Amherst MA: University of Massachusetts, 1993.
Lincoln, Eleanor Terry and John Abel Pinto, *This, The House We Live In: The Smith College Campus from 1871 to 1982,* Northampton MA: Smith College, 1983.
MacMillan, John, "The Simmons Years: Vision and Inspiration," *Smith Alumnae Quarterly,* vol. 87, no. 3, (Spring 2001): 20–21.
Millman, Rachel, "A building grows out of a path" *The Sophian,* (May 15, 2003): 3.
Peabody, Robert S. Letters. Society for the Protection of New England Antiquities.
—"A Talk About Queen Anne" *The American Architect and Building News* (April 28, 1877): 133–34.
Pearson, Clifford A., "Weiss/Manfredi integrate the Modern Smith College Campus Center into its historic and natural setting." *Architectural Record,* v. 192, no. 8, (August 2004): 112–119.
Sawyer, Philip, "Early Days of York and Sawyer," *Journal of the American Institute of Architects,* (Nov. 16, 1951): 195–200.
Schmidt, Anne Carlisle, "The Cutter Ziskind Complex: Modern Architecture at Smith College," thesis submitted to the Department of Art, Smith College, (April, 1992):100, Undergraduate Student Papers, Drawer 1.
Schneider, Gretchen, "The Evolving Landscape of the Smith Campus." *NewsSmith* (Fall 2005): 12
Searing, Helen, "A History of the Art Buildings at Smith College." *Image and Word: Art and Art History at Smith College.* Northampton MA: Smith College, 2003.
Seelye, L. Clark. *Annual Report of the President of Smith College, 1898–1899.* Northampton MA: Smith College, 1899.
—"Inaugural Address," *Addresses at the Inauguration of Rev. L. Clark Seelye as President of Smith College, and at the Dedication of Its Academic Building, July 14, 1875.* Springfield MA: Clark W. Bryan & Co. 1875.

—*The Early History of Smith College 1871–1910*. Boston & New York: Houghton Mifflin Co. 1923. Smith College Archives

Taylor, Phoebe, "Men's Lodgings." *The Sophian* (Nov. 6, 1969): 4.

Thorpe, Margaret Farrand, *Neilson of Smith*, New York: Oxford University Press, 1956.

Vickery, Margaret Birney, *Buildings for Bluestockings: The Architecture and Social History of Women's Colleges in Late Victorian England*, Newark: University of Delaware Press & London: Associated University Presses. 1999.

Weir, Emily Harrison, "Hail (and Farewell) Mary Dunn," *NewsSmith*, (Spring 1995): 1, 4–7.

Weld, Eric Sean, "Working Towards a Sustainable Campus," *NewsSmith*, (Fall, 2005): 1, 6–8.

Index

(Italics indicate a photograph. Main descriptive sections are in boldface.)